M000200801

GET REAL

Bill Myers

HARVEST HOUSE PUBLISHERS

EUGENE, OREGON

Unless otherwise indicated, all Scripture quotations are taken from the Holy Bible: New International Version®. NIV®. Copyright © 1973, 1978, 1984 by the International Bible Society. Used by permission of Zondervan Publishing House. The "NIV" and "New International Version" trademarks are registered in the United States Patent and Trademark Office by International Bible Society.

Verses marked NASB are taken from the New American Standard Bible ®, © 1960, 1962, 1963, 1968, 1971, 1972, 1973, 1975, 1977 by The Lockman Foundation. Used by permission.

Verses marked KJV are taken from the King James Version of the Bible.

All italics used in Scripture quotations are added for emphasis by the author.

Published in association with the literary agency of Alive Communications, Inc., 7680 Goddard Street, Suite 200, Colorado Springs, CO 80920.

Portions of this material were previously published as *Faith Workout* (Scripture Press, 1986).

Cover by Left Coast Design, Portland, Oregon

Cover photos © Fancy Photography/Veer; Image Source/Workbook

GET REAL
Formerly titled *Just Believe It*
Copyright © 2001 by Bill Myers
Published by Harvest House Publishers
Eugene, Oregon 97402
www.harvesthousepublishers.com

Library of Congress Cataloging-in-Publication Data

Myers, Bill, 1953–
  [Just belive it]
  Get real / Bill Myers.
    p. cm.
  Originally published: Just believe it. Eugene, Or.: Harvest House Publishers, c2001.
  ISBN-13: 978-0-7369-1682-0 (pbk.)
  ISBN-10: 0-7369-1682-2 (pbk.)
  1. Bible. N.T. James—Commentaries I. Title.
  BS2785.53.M94 2005
  227'.91077—dc22   2005018860

All rights reserved. No part of this publication may be reproduced, stored in a retrieval system, or transmitted in any form or by any means—electronic, mechanical, digital, photocopy, recording, or any other—except for brief quotations in printed reviews, without the prior permission of the publisher.

Printed in the United States of America

06 07 08 09 10 11 12 / VP-CF / 10 9 8 7 6 5 4 3 2 1

For Nichole and Mackenzie—

As you continue to become
"mature and complete, not lacking anything."

Contents

A Couple Things to Note Before We Start...

1. God's Word Is Powerful

God's Word is the most powerful weapon that has ever existed. When Satan was tempting Jesus in the desert—when the most evil force in the universe was battling the Creator of the universe—they didn't use guns, bombs, or lasers. They didn't even try to nuke one another. They both knew the ultimate weapon and used it. They both fought with God's Holy Word, the Bible.

There's something supernatural about God's Word. First of all, it's "God-breathed" (2 Timothy 3:16). Imagine, God actually breathed His very life into the words of Scripture.

And because it has His life, as we read His Word it changes us...from the inside. Here's a short list of some of the other things reading the Word does for us:

☞ It cleanses us (Ephesians 5:26).

☞ It helps us to see ourselves as we really are (James 1:23-25).

☞ It encourages us (Romans 15:4).

☞ It equips us to do good (2 Timothy 3:17).

☞ It gives us faith (Romans 10:17).

☞ It can actually help save us (James 1:21).

Pretty powerful stuff. And not something to be taken lightly.

So don't race through this book. Take your time. Let it do its work. In fact, try to read just one section per sitting.

After you've looked over the Scripture portion at the top of each section, stop a moment to see what God is telling you. Don't plow through and read my commentary until you've taken a moment to see if He is saying anything to you personally. Then, after you've waited, go ahead and read the commentary. Just remember that as helpful as the commentary may be, it's important that you always put God's Word first. What I have to say is human opinion, though I try to make sure I am in line with His Word. Put His Word first, and you'll do well.

2. God's Word Is Straightforward

The Book of James is no-nonsense and straight to the point. It never candy-coats things or makes them easy to swallow. If something's wrong, it tells us. If we're not meeting God's standards, it lets us know.

This is great, but it can also be a little hard to take.

As you read, you'll come across sections that will apply to your particular areas of weakness. You may feel the guilt piling on or start to become discouraged or even begin to lose hope.

That's an old trick of the enemy's. Don't fall for it. The purpose of James' letter and this book is to help instruct and encourage you, not clobber you over the head with guilt and hopelessness.

The point is that God would not bring up these areas in your life if He didn't *know* you'd be able to lick them.

That's what the Book of James is all about—to point out the problem areas so the two of you can get together and start working on them.

That's right, the two of you. You're not in this alone. God is on your side (not a bad teammate). And together you can work through any problem. As you remain with Jesus and allow Him to do His work in you, you'll begin to see His purpose in your life being accomplished. You'll begin to see yourself becoming "mature and complete, not lacking anything" (James 1:4).

1
FAITH ON TRIAL

Who?

James, a bond-servant of God and of the Lord Jesus Christ, to the twelve tribes who are dispersed abroad, greetings.
JAMES 1:1 NASB

No doubt this was James the disciple, right? The guy who followed Jesus around for those three years. The one who got mad at the Samaritans and wanted to call down fire from the sky to wipe them out. The man who was with Peter and John when Jesus had His chat on the mountain with Moses and Elijah. No doubt this was the same James, right?

Wrong.

According to most scholars, this was an entirely different James. This James had some important family connections...

He was Jesus' brother!

That's right. (Well, actually, they were only half brothers because James' father was Joseph and Jesus' Father is

God.) But can you imagine growing up with a brother who just happens to be the Son of God? I mean, we may have brothers or sisters who always *think* they're right; but when Jesus was right, **HE WAS RIGHT!** In fact, according to Scripture, Jesus was perfect. He never sinned. He never did *anything* wrong.

Now let's face it, at times that must have been a pain. I mean, how do you win an argument with someone when He just happens to be God the Son?

But look at how James begins his letter. We would probably start off with something like this:

James, Jesus' favorite brother, who always let Him use my bike, who always let Him have first dibs on borrowing Dad's car, who roomed with Him for 18 years, and who probably knows Him better than anyone else alive...

But not James. He uses only one word to describe his special relationship with Jesus:

"Bond-servant" (a polite word for "slave").

Talk about humility. Instead of trying to impress us with his family ties, he simply refers to himself as a slave of God and Jesus Christ.

Not that it was always that way. Back in John 7:5 we see that "even his own brothers did not believe in him." In fact, in Mark 3:21 we read that at one point Jesus' family actually tried to "take charge of him, for they said, 'He is out of his mind.'"

Seems kind of strange. How could a person hang around Jesus all those years watching Him heal the sick, raise people from the dead, and dramatically change lives, yet never really believe?

But then again, how many people today hang around the church all their lives, watching others being changed, while they never really make a serious commitment themselves? Oh, they're there every Sunday, know most of the songs, know when to sit and when to stand—they have the whole routine covered. But when it comes down to the real stuff, when it comes down to the decision to really giving Christ 100 percent control, how many hold back, not really believing, afraid that if they give Him everything, He'll somehow mess up?

But isn't that what He wants? To be in charge of everything? Not because He's some sort of egotist, but when He's in charge, when He's our Lord or boss 100 percent of the time, He'll make sure *we* don't mess up. He'll make sure we don't settle for second rate. He'll make sure He's always there to help us taste and experience life at its fullest. To live the type of life He dreamed we would live when He first created us.

It's a scary thought to put someone else in charge (even if it is God), but eventually that's what James did. No one is sure when, but somewhere along the line he went through an *incredible* change. Somewhere along the line he took the chance and decided to "go all the way" with the Lord. Somewhere along the line he was willing to become God's slave.

And it wasn't too long before he wound up in charge of the whole church in Jerusalem (see Acts 15). No small deal.

It was probably when he held that position that he wrote this letter to all the believers outside Jerusalem. As a leader he had seen the tremendous victories of his fellow Christians, as well as their heartbreaking defeats.

So with the guidance and direction of the Holy Spirit, he set out to give some solid, practical advice. No doubt he was hoping it would be a guide—a road map to help us through dark valleys and over insurmountable mountains so we can always experience victory…

Always.

PONDERING POINTS

☞ Have you given God total control of your life?

☞ What are you holding back?

☞ Why?

☞ If He really loves you and if He's really on your side, do those reasons hold up?

Why Pain?

*Consider it pure joy, my brothers, whenever you face trials of
many kinds, because you know that the testing of your faith
develops perseverance. Perseverance must finish its work so
that you may be mature and complete, not lacking anything.*
JAMES 1:2-4

Somehow, some of us may have the impression that once
we became Christians, life would be a piece of cake. No
problems, no headaches—we just sort of sit back and
cruise to heaven.

Nice idea, but not exactly what the Lord has in mind.
Instead of sitting nice and cozy up in the bleachers,
chowing down on hot dogs and popcorn, we suddenly
find ourselves down on the track, working out!

Trials come. They come in all shapes and sizes, from
little irritations to mega-heartaches. They seem baffling,
confusing. You may even find yourself falling into the ol'
"If God really loves me, why is He letting this happen to
me?" routine.

And that's the answer:

**God lets all those things happen to you
because He loves you.**

Say what?

That's right. You see, you only own one thing that's
eternal. You're only taking one thing to heaven: yourself.

That's it. The cars, the grades, the relationships, the jobs—none of those things count in the long run.

People. You and me. We're the only things that are important, the only things that are eternal.

So God takes that one important element, you, and begins to give you a workout—to exercise and to build your muscles, to run you around the track again and again and again some more. And then—when you're sure you can't take another step—He gives you one more lap. Not because He's some sort of dictator, but because He loves you. In the end He wants you to really be happy, to "be mature and complete, not lacking anything."

But James doesn't let it go at that. He doesn't just say, "OK, guys, try your best not to complain or mutter when trials come your way." He actually takes it a step further. His command to us is:

"Consider it *pure* joy."

He's got to be kidding!

Nope. You see, there's some sort of truth here that he's trying to clue us in on. If, as Christians, we could begin to look on pain as actually being something that's good for us—as an athlete does when he's working out—if we could begin to understand that tough times are not supposed to flatten us, but that they are supposed to strengthen us and help us become winners, then we could see things from a totally different perspective.

We could actually begin to welcome pain. Or, as the Bible says, "always giving thanks for all things" (Ephesians 5:20 NASB). We could really begin to understand that "God causes all things to work together for good to those who love God, to those who are called according to His purpose" (Romans 8:28 NASB).

Life isn't always a piece of cake. In fact, sometimes it can be a real pain. The trick is to figure out how the hard times can help you, how they can make you better, how they can make you more like Jesus, "mature and complete, not lacking *anything.*"

PONDERING POINTS

☞ What tough stuff are you going through?

☞ How could God use it to make you more like Jesus? (The trick is not to ask *why* something's happening, but *how* God can use it.)

☞ Try worshiping Him and thanking Him—not for the hard stuff, but that He's still in charge and will somehow use that hard stuff "to work together for the good" if you hang in there and love Him.

Wisdom

If any of you lacks wisdom, he should ask God, who gives generously to all without finding fault, and it will be given to him.
JAMES 1:5

Way back in 1 Kings 3, the Lord appeared to King Solomon and told him he could have whatever he asked for. Instead of asking for riches or health or fame, Solomon went for something entirely different. He asked for *wisdom*.

God was so pleased with that request that He not only gave him wisdom, but He threw in everything else as well. Why? What's the big deal about wisdom?

Wisdom is seeing things from God's perspective.

Sometimes you're so close to a situation you can't see the whole picture the way He can.

Trials are a good example. Sometimes you get so bummed about a particular problem you forget it's for your own good. You can't possibly see how you're supposed to grow from flunking a test, losing a good friend, or coming in last place.

That's where wisdom fits in.

Wisdom is God showing you the situation from His eternal point of view. It's showing you how everything fits—how you're supposed to pray, what you're supposed to do, how you can overcome the problem, and most important, how that problem can help you grow. Without wisdom you'd be bumping into one wall after another until you just happened to stumble through the doorway of His will.

That's what the "big deal" is.

And how do you get wisdom?

Ask.

Despite the rumors, God is not some sort of sadist who plays hide and seek with His will. If you ask, you'll receive wisdom. It's as simple as that. He's into giving, remember? He's not going to look for faults and excuses to withhold it. He's on your side. He *wants* to help.

But when He gives wisdom, it usually isn't with fireworks or writing on the wall. Instead, as you continue to ask, day in and day out, you begin to somehow know what He would have you do. Day after day, as you spend time with the Lord, you begin to see the situation from His perspective.

It's like being around a very close friend. Gradually, as you spend more and more time together, you begin thinking alike. Then eventually you begin to find yourselves saying or doing some of the same things—not because you're trying to imitate each other, but because you've grown so close.

The same is true with the Lord. In this day of fast food and getting anything you want when you want it, some people expect God to work the same way. All you have to do is drop in a coin, press the prayer button, and out pops instant wisdom. But that doesn't seem to be His style. Oh, He'll help out if you get into a jam and need an immediate rescue. But He seems to prefer the slower, day-by-day style.

Each day as you spend time with Him, you slowly begin to see and think as He does. And seeing and thinking as He does—that's having wisdom.

PONDERING POINTS

☞ Why is wisdom better than anything else to ask for?

☞ What things in your life would you like to see from God's perspective?

Making Decisions

But when he asks, he must believe and not doubt, because he who doubts is like a wave of the sea, blown and tossed by the wind. That man should not think he will receive anything from the Lord; he is a double-minded man, unstable in all he does.
JAMES 1:6-8

So you've got a tough decision to make. Either choice will have some good in it as well as some bad. What you need is a good, healthy dose of wisdom. What do you do?

First, decide if you want to do what God wants. If you do, no matter how hard it may seem, then you've already got it figured out. You may not have the answer yet, but the question is solved.

Come again?

God promises:

The steps of a good man are ordered by the Lord.
Psalm 37:23 KJV

If you are truly seeking His will in a situation, He'll literally point your feet in the direction He wants you to go. All you have to do is be willing to do His will, ask for wisdom, and step out.

But I still have to make the decision!

That's right. But rest assured that whatever you decide, that very decision will be the one God intends for you to make. Not because you're some sort of genius, but because *He* will be directing your thoughts.

23

I doubt you'll get any angel-grams or find answers carved in stone. You still have to use common sense, make a list of the pros and cons, do a little research, and talk with people you respect. But once that's done and you've prayed about it, *the decision you finally come up with will be the one the Lord wants you to make.*

Sorry it's so easy, but that's the truth.

The problems come when you start to doubt. If you ask in faith, you're OK. But when you start to doubt that He'll really answer, you become like a wave in a stormy sea—tossed this way and that, back and forth, one minute thinking this, the next minute thinking that. You become frustrated, confused—a real mess. We've all been through it.

James described it best as double-mindedness, when the ol' thoughts start to war against one another inside your head. "Should I do this or that?" And, as James says, you can get so tied up that you actually receive nothing from the Lord. A process that was designed to be easy for His children can turn into a nightmare, a situation in which you are so paralyzed you're afraid to make any move.

Don't let that happen. If you've sought the Lord and asked for wisdom, then just *believe* you've received it (whether you feel particularly brainy or not). And even if you've made a mistake, He'll turn it around for the best.

He's used to having His way—especially with those He wants to protect, especially with those He loves.

Especially with those He loves.

PONDERING POINTS

☞ In the old days boat captains used to know they were in the channel of a harbor when they lined up three strategically placed lights on a hill so closely that the three lights appeared as one. The same can be true for us. If we use God's Word as one light, the counsel we receive from mature Christians as another, and our own gut feelings from the Holy Spirit, and if all three line up, then we know we're on course. If they don't line up, then consider waiting. God may have an entirely different solution in mind. Most mistakes are made because we're too hasty. God will always make His will clear in His time.

Always.

2
REAL RICHES

Say What?

The brother in humble circumstances ought to take pride in his high position.
JAMES 1:9

At first glance this sort of double-talk sounds like James is practicing to run for political office.

But what he's saying is true…strange, but true. A while back a guy from our youth group asked: "Why can't I hold off becoming a Christian until I know I'm going to die? That way I can have all the fun I want now, and then at the last minute I can slip in under the wire."

He had a good point. Now, while he was young, why couldn't he party, drink, have sex, do drugs, and just generally have a "good time"? Then later, when he was older, he could repent and "get saved."

The trouble is that such "good times" always spell pain. Oh, they may be fun for a while, but they're just like a baited hook. On the outside it looks great, but once you swallow it, Satan starts reeling you in, controlling you, stealing your real joy, robbing you of real peace and real happiness.

And it's these gifts—joy, peace, and happiness—that make you rich. These are what the rest of the world is really after as they gobble down those baited hooks.

But according to Jesus, you can have these gifts for free. It makes no difference how little money, popularity, or natural talent you have. These are the gifts that really make your life rich. These are the gifts that God offers to each of His kids: Joy...peace...happiness.

Jesus said:

**I came that they might have life,
and might have it *abundantly*.**
John 10:10 NASB

But there's another reason for becoming a Christian early on: you get involved in God's training program. He trains you not only to develop the eternal character we've already talked about, but also to prepare you to rule the universe.

Excuse me?

That's right. According to Scripture, you and I will actually help Christ run the universe!

Find that a bit hard to swallow? Take a look at these verses:

**To him who overcomes, I will give
the right to sit with me on my throne.**
Revelation 3:21

Now if we are children, then we are heirs—heirs of God and co-heirs with Christ, if indeed we share in his sufferings in order that we may also share in his glory.
Romans 8:17

In fact, according to the Bible, you and I will actually judge angels!

Do you not know that the saints [that's us] will judge the world?…Do you not know that we will judge angels?
1 Corinthians 6:2,3

No wonder James tells us to take pride in our high position! Out of all creation, God has chosen us to corule the universe with Him. Out of all creation, He has chosen us to be His children…to "share in His glory."

PONDERING POINTS

☞ What areas in your life should God strengthen before you are ready to help Him run the universe?

☞ How do you think He'll help you strengthen those areas?

So You Wanna Be Rich

But the one who is rich should take pride in his low position, because he will pass away like a wild flower. For the sun rises with scorching heat and withers the plant; its blossom falls and its beauty is destroyed. In the same way, the rich man will fade away even while he goes about his business.
JAMES 1:10,11

The "scorching heat" James talks about could very well be a *simoon*—a fiery wind that comes roaring out of the desert. It is so hot and fierce that in one hour it can completely wipe out plant life.

That's how easily riches can be destroyed. That's how vulnerable they are. And even if you manage to make it through life without losing them, there's still no way you can take them to heaven. After all, when was the last time you saw a U-Haul following a hearse to the cemetery?

Still, people spend their whole lives trying to earn that extra dollar—stepping on others, lying, cheating, looking out for number one, ignoring loved ones. They think if they can get enough money and buy all the "toys," they'll somehow be safe, happy, and secure.

Now there's nothing wrong with money. Don't get me wrong—I'm into eating as much as the next guy. But as soon as you start putting it ahead of serving God or serving others, as soon as getting that car or saving for college becomes more important than helping somebody, then you're in trouble. In fact, it was Jesus Himself who said:

No servant can serve two masters.
Either he will hate the one and love the other,
or he will be devoted to the one and despise the other.
You cannot serve both God and Money.
Luke 16:13

And as much as we'd like to prove Him wrong, as much as we'd like to believe it wouldn't happen with us, Jesus says it always will. We cannot chase after money and chase after God.

It's one or the other, not both.

Don't worry, though. He promises that if you seek Him first, He'll always provide what you need.

But seek first his kingdom and his righteousness,
and all these things will be given to you as well.
Matthew 6:33

And being rich isn't such a hot deal.

I know, I know, you're thinking if richness is a problem, may God strike you with it so bad that you never recover.

But listen: Besides worrying about who's trying to get your money and how they're going to get it, if you're rich you may find yourself starting to trust your bank account more than God. And if that gets to be too big of a problem, then in that deep love of His that wants you to be made perfect and complete, God will look for other ways to help you start trusting again—like through your health, your friends, your loved ones.

Because if He didn't bring you back to trusting Him, you could get to the point where you wouldn't even trust Him for your salvation. And then you'd really be in hot water.

Maybe that's what Jesus meant when He said, "It is easier for a camel to go through the eye of a needle than for a rich man to enter the kingdom of God" (Matthew 19:24).

And maybe, just maybe, wise old Solomon knew what he was talking about when he said, "Give me neither poverty nor riches, but give me only my daily bread. Otherwise, I may have too much and disown you and say, 'Who is the LORD?'" (Proverbs 30:8,9).

PONDERING POINTS

☞ What areas compete with God as riches in your life?

☞ What can you do to make sure they won't rule over you?

Crown of Life

Blessed is the man who perseveres under trial, because when he has stood the test, he will receive the crown of life that God has promised to those who love him.
JAMES 1:12

Silver is a wonderful metal. In its purest form it's bright, beautiful, and used in some of the world's finest jewelry. But it doesn't come out of the ground that way.

When it's first discovered, it's mixed with plenty of rock and useless ore. The potential for its beauty is there, but in the beginning it's not much to look at.

The same is true with us. God sees us as precious metal. But like silver, we have a long way to go before we start to look like anything.

We need to go through some…
you guessed it…testing.

The process used to bring out the beauty in silver is fairly simple. The refiner dumps the ore into the furnace and heats it up. This removes all the worthless rock and debris from the metal. But he doesn't do it just once. He heats up that furnace again and again and again.

Each time the heat removes more of the impurities, enabling the silver to become more pure, more precious.

But how does the refiner know when the metal has reached its purest, most precious state? When he is able to look down into it and see a perfect reflection of his face.

And that's how the Lord works with you. He allows you to be tested and refined, strengthened and matured until He can look at you and see Himself.

He doesn't do this because He's some sort of egotist or because He wants a bunch of Jesus clones walking around. He allows the refining because when you are like Christ, you have reached your fullest and greatest potential. You have become your strongest, happiest, most complete self. You have become God's precious and most beautiful handiwork, fit to help Him rule His universe.

That's the crown of life James is talking about. If you persevere under the trials, if you stand the tests, you will receive that crown—a crown given to victors, a crown given only to royalty.

PONDERING POINTS

☞ What areas in your life need to be heated up and removed?

☞ Do you think God will do it?

☞ How?

It's Not My Fault!

Let no one say when he is tempted, "I am being tempted by God"; for God cannot be tempted by evil, and He Himself does not tempt anyone.
JAMES 1:13 NASB

As humans we love to pass the buck...

"Don't look at me—it wasn't my fault!"

"He started it!"

Or as Adam so aptly put it: "The woman you put here with me—she gave me some fruit from the tree" (Genesis 3:12).

And of course, let's not forget Eve's great defense: "The serpent deceived me" (Genesis 3:13).

Everyone's to blame but us. And if we can't find anybody else, there's always God.

This is the mentality that James is trying to clear up. If we sin, if we give in to temptation, let's 'fess up to it and move along. Let's not dump it on God—as if He's up there thinking of ways to trick us and make us stumble and fall.

He's not the one who gets us into heavy make out sessions with our dates. He's not the one who gets us to dis our friends, or tell our parents to drop dead, or cheat on tests.

He's on our side.

But we load the revolver, point it to our heads, and say, "If You really love me, God, when I pull the trigger it won't go off." And if it does..."Well it certainly wasn't my fault because God is all-powerful and could have stopped me if He really wanted to."

It's true that He's all-powerful—but He's also into free will. If we insist on jumping off a cliff, He'll do His best to warn us of the consequences. But if we still insist, He'll respect us enough to let us have our way...even if it means watching His children that He deeply loves destroy themselves.

And while we're on the subject of blaming God...

What about all these tests and trials we've been talking about, the ones designed to make us "mature and complete, not lacking anything." Is He to blame for those?

Does He wake up in the morning and, after a hearty stretch and yawn, decide which one of His kids He's going to clobber today?

Not quite.

Remember, He is on your side. He bought you with everything He had—His very life. He's not about to abuse or neglect something that has cost Him so much and is so precious to Him.

Most of our hard times come as a result of sin. If not our sin, then somebody else's. Even sickness and death originated with sin. (We were designed to live forever, till Adam ate the fruit.) It's true that God could get in there and stop the bad times, especially when they involve a so-called innocent party. But then He'd be accused of "meddling" and not giving us our free will.

So instead, He has allowed man and Satan to play out their hands and have their own way...for a while. But eventually He'll take what has been done and start turning it around for good. He'll either show us how to take authority over our circumstances through faith and prayer, or He'll let the tough times strengthen and mature us.

Either way, He puts Romans 8:28 into play:

All things work together for good to them that love God… (KJV).

All this to say: God is on your side. When you are being tempted or tested, turn to Him for help, not blame.

PONDERING POINTS

☞ In what areas of your life do you pass the buck?

☞ What would God do if you took ownership of them?

3

BEATING TEMPTATION

The Sin Process

But each one is tempted when he is carried away and enticed by his own lust. Then when lust has conceived, it gives birth to sin; and when sin is accomplished, it brings forth death.
JAMES 1:14,15 NASB

We like sin.

Let's face it. When something is forbidden, we're no different than Adam and Eve. We want to know why it's forbidden; we want to know what we're losing out on and if it's really as much fun as everybody says. In short, if you really want to want something, just have someone tell you that you can't have it.

It's strange, but that's how we're wired. We're born with this desire, this lust. It's genetic, coming from thousands of years of sin in our race.

But we also hate sin.

If you've asked Jesus to forgive you and come inside to take charge over that "old sin nature," then there's part of you that now hates to sin. And when you do sin, you feel guilty, discouraged, and cut off from God.

So in essence what you have is a civil war raging inside your head—the old part of you wanting to sin, the Jesus part wanting to do right. Sometimes you win, sometimes you lose.

But there is a way to win every single time— if you really want to.

Sin has been described as a bird trying to nest in a tree. If the tree were to shake off the bird every time it tried to land, the bird eventually would fly away. But if the tree lets the bird stay, the bird will eventually build a nest and hatch its young.

The same is true with us. Thoughts of sin frequently come in and bombard our minds. That's only normal. Those thoughts aren't sin—they're only temptation. The sin comes when we refuse to shake those thoughts out of our heads, when we refuse to take authority over them. We let them live inside—thinking about them over and over again until finally, almost before we know it, the thoughts give birth to action.

The trick is to shake off those *thoughts* of temptation before they have time to take root. Don't dwell on them. Don't drool over them like some kid at a candy counter. If you really don't want them around, then take authority over them and tell them to leave in Jesus' name. And they will.

But not for long.

They'll keep coming back, testing you to see if you're really serious. If you are, you'll keep demanding that they leave. And they will...until finally they never return. If you're not serious, you'll eventually give in and allow them to stay, which *inevitably* leads to sin.

But the choice is always yours.

You are not a mindless puppet. You are a creature of free will. And if you are a Christian, you have extra help. You have Jesus Christ living inside, giving you the power to resist temptation. But only if that's what you want.

And it's in that "if"—your free will—that the final decision will be made.

PONDERING POINTS

☞ Are there any sins that you don't want to give over to Jesus?

☞ Why?

☞ What would happen if you did give them over?

☞ How would you feel in the long run?

God's Gifts

Do not be deceived, my beloved brethren. Every good thing bestowed and every perfect gift is from above, coming down from the Father of lights, with whom there is no variation, or shifting shadow. In the exercise of His will He brought us forth by the word of truth, so that we might be, as it were, the first fruits among His creatures.
JAMES 1:16-18 NASB

Once again, James makes it clear that we're clueless if we think God is the one who tempts us to do evil or that He clobbers us with trials.

It's just the opposite.

God is responsible for the good—He's the One to thank for the "perfect gifts."

Satan would love for us to get that truth mixed up and start blaming God for the bad. And a lot of people fall for that con job with the old "If God is a God of love, how come He allowed such and such to happen?"

But we humans have been telling God to butt out of our business for the last 6,000 years. And honoring our free will, He does just that—but only for a little while. Eventually He comes in, takes all the bad, and turns it around to good. But only for those who want Him to, for those who love Him and are doing what He asks. "We know that in all things God works for the good of those who love him, who have been called according to his purpose" (Romans 8:28).

James goes on to explain that God—who created the stars, moon, and sun—doesn't change like the shadows they cast, shadows that shift from hour to hour.

God's not like that.

In this age everything is changing so fast. What's in today is cliché tomorrow, what's morally offensive today will be the norm tomorrow. But...

Amidst all this change, it's good to know that God stays the same. He will not change. What He said thousands of years ago still stands today.

He's our Rock, the very foundation we build our lives on. And today, more than ever, it's good to know that Rock will *never* move or be shaken. His Word will always hold true.

He will cause all things to work together for good to those who love and follow Him.

Not some things, not most things, but *all* things.

PONDERING POINTS

☞ What moral changes in our society have you seen during your lifetime?

☞ How have those changes affected you?

☞ How have they affected God and His truth?

Be Cool

My dear brothers, take note of this: Everyone should be quick to listen, slow to speak and slow to become angry, for man's anger does not bring about the righteous life that God desires.
JAMES 1:19,20

There's something else about us humans. Why do we always do stupid things when we're angry? Could somebody tell me that?

You can take the brightest, most "reasonable" person in the world, but when he gets angry and acts out of that anger, watch out. He'll always look and sound like a AAA, certified *jerk*.

Proverbs is full of comments about people who don't control their tempers and people who do:

**A fool shows his annoyance at once,
but a prudent man overlooks an insult.**
Proverbs 12:16

A quick-tempered man does foolish things.
Proverbs 14:17

**A patient man has great understanding, but a
quick-tempered man displays folly.**
Proverbs 14:29

Do not make friends with a hot-tempered man, do not associate with one easily angered, or you may learn his ways and get yourself ensnared.
Proverbs 22:24,25

He who is slow to anger is better than the mighty, and he who rules his spirit, than he who captures a city.
Proverbs 16:32 NASB

And the list goes on.

So basically what James says along with the rest of Scripture is, "If you want to come off smart, be cool." But how do you do it? How do you keep from exploding and looking stupid?

The trick is to listen patiently to what the other person says and not to leap at him with a snappy comeback or put-down. Even if what they say or do really bugs you, let it sit for a while.

When you're sure you're not answering out of anger, then respond. Chances are you'll look like less of a jerk than the other guy. And who knows? If you're careful to listen, you may just find out the other guy has a halfway decent point.

What if my temper really stinks?

Well, that makes things tougher but not impossible. Remember that free will we talked about? Nothing, absolutely nothing, can control you if you don't want it to. The same goes for your temper. You can control it. It may take some work and a whole lot of prayer, but with God's help you can control it...if you really want to.

If that's an area you need to work on, ask the Lord to make you sensitive to it and to give you the power to control it.

And then be prepared…He'll probably take you through the ol' training grounds of testings and trials.

When you start facing those little flare-ups, when your blood begins to heat up, immediately ask the Lord for help. He'll be there every time. It may not feel like it, but He'll always be there to help—if you really want that help.

And there will be times you won't want it. There will be times you really want to fail. And guess what? You will. But don't grow discouraged. We all go through those times no matter what we're fighting. It's usually two steps forward and one back. Sometimes the progress may seem unbearably slow, sometimes terribly discouraging.

But you'll always move forward. And eventually you'll win. Because the Coach will always be at your side. Because He wants you to be happy. Because, more than anything else, He wants His children to be "mature and complete, not lacking anything."

PONDERING POINTS

☞ When's the last time you really blew your cool?

☞ When it was over, how did you feel?

☞ What would you have done differently to keep your cool?

Condensed Food

Therefore, get rid of all moral filth and the evil that is so prevalent and humbly accept the word planted in you, which can save you.
JAMES 1:21

In this single sentence James manages to make three very important points.

First, get rid of the crud. Not some of it, not most of it, but *all* of it. All of the stuff we say, think, and do that we know is wrong but go ahead and do anyway.

It's interesting that he doesn't say, "Why don't you *try* to give it up?" or "That's OK, we all sin, don't worry about it." He doesn't give us that option. Instead, God's Holy Word says:

GET RID OF IT!

And again, we can…if we ask for God's help and we really want to. It'll take time and probably mean going through God's training program. But if we hang in there, the final result will be that we are, you guessed it, "mature and complete, not lacking anything."

Second, as mentioned in the introduction, there is something powerfully supernatural about God's Word. In 2 Timothy 3:16 we read that "all Scripture is inspired by God" (NASB) and by inspired, it doesn't mean the writer got all excited about God and wrote something inspirational. No. A more accurate translation is that all Scripture is "God breathed." Think of that. The words in your Bible have the very breath of God in them!

During Paul's whole description about the "armor of God" in Ephesians 6, our only offensive weapon is the Word of God. All the other weapons of warfare mentioned there are strictly for defense. But not God's Word. It's our sword. It's what we use to defeat the enemy.

Again, when Jesus, the Creator of the universe, and Satan, the most evil creature in the universe, fought in the wilderness, they didn't use tanks, lasers, or nuclear weapons. Instead, they fought with what they knew to be the most powerful weapon: the Word of God. Because...

**The Word of God is living and active.
[It is] sharper than any double-edged sword...**
Hebrews 4:12

God's Word is also seed that is planted inside our hearts. And if we allow it to take root, that seed will grow and mature and be fruitful.

Third, be teachable. Let God and His Word work in your heart. Don't fight Him. Don't argue. Don't try to defend yourself. If He corrects you, accept it. If you mess up, admit it. He'll forgive you. He's not going to bang you over the head. He's on your side. And because He loves you, He'll eventually have His way with you anyway, so why not give in to Him now and avoid the rush?

Being teachable is like being quality clay in the Potter's hands. If you're soft and pliable, He can easily form you into the marvelous work of art He intends for you to be.

If you're stiff-necked and stubborn—if the clay is hard and brittle—it's going to take a lot more time and effort. Pieces will snap off, and there will be a lot of pain.

Stay pliable. Not only is it faster, it's a whole lot easier.

PONDERING POINTS

☞ What "moral filth" are you dealing with?

☞ How could you let God help you get rid of it?

4
DO IT

The Great Deception

*Do not merely listen to the word, and so deceive yourselves. Do
what it says. Anyone who listens to the word but does not do
what it says is like a man who looks at his face in a mirror and,
after looking at himself, goes away and immediately forgets
what he looks like.*
JAMES 1:22-24

Harold was a good kid. He got good grades, was con-
siderate of others, and caused his parents as little grief as
possible. In short, he was an all right guy. Harold only had
one little problem: he thought he was a BMW.

Every night he would sleep in the garage because, after
all, isn't that where expensive automobiles spend the
night? And whenever people tried to reason with him, he
would point out that because he stayed in the garage it
was proof he really was a car. His mom and dad would go
out and plead with him, tying to get him to see reason. He
never acted like a car—never needed his oil changed or

his tires rotated. And when was the last time he felt the need for a tune-up?

They even brought out a mirror so he could see for himself. When he looked into it, he had to admit he didn't look much like a car. But whenever they removed the mirror, he immediately forgot what he looked like and again insisted that he was a BMW.

Try as they might, his parents could not get him to see reason. Though it was a difficult decision, they eventually had to trade him in for a new family van.

An absurd story? Of course. But how many people are like ol' Harold? They figure because they sit in a church it automatically makes them a Christian. They've always listened to the teachings of Jesus Christ. But because they never got around to asking Him to forgive them and take control of their lives, they're no more a Christian than Harold is a BMW.

Let's bring it a little closer to home…

Many of us sit in church, listen to what the Bible says about something, and nod our heads saying, "Yup, that's right." But we never do what it says. Does that make us any different from Harold? Wouldn't the best test to prove if Harold was a car be for his family to climb inside him and drive him across the state to visit Aunt Clara? If he really was a car, wouldn't that be the ultimate proof?

If we're really Christians, shouldn't the ultimate proof be in what we do—not what we say or where we sit, but whether we really do what the Bible teaches?

That's what James is saying here:

Don't just sit around and listen to the Word. Do it.

He goes on to make another point…

Because God loves you and wants you complete, another quality of His Word is its ability to act as a mirror. When you read it, it helps you take a good look at yourself—to see where you're succeeding and where you're falling short. Its purpose is not to condemn you, but to show you where you need help so you can turn to Him for that help.

But according to James:

**Many people read God's Word, see where they're
falling short, then close the book
and go about their merry way.**

They completely forget about the areas that need work—about the areas God wants them to be mature in. They are like a guy who looks into a mirror and sees that his face is caked with mud, then forgets to clean it.

PONDERING POINTS

☞ What are areas of disobedience in your life?

☞ What does the Word say about them?

☞ What are you going to do about them?

☞ What will happen if you don't?

Formula for Success

But the man who looks intently into the perfect law that gives freedom, and continues to do this, not forgetting what he has heard, but doing it—he will be blessed in what he does.
JAMES 1:25

Just as there are some who look into the Word of God, see themselves, then forget to do anything, there are also others who do something about what they see. They carefully study God's Word and then apply it to their lives. According to James, these people will be "blessed"— successful in whatever they do.

Sounds good, but does it really work?

I heard of one fellow who thinks it does. Like most Christians, he had listened to and read about Jesus' continual emphasis on helping others. He knew about treating others as he would want to be treated and serving others regardless of the cost to himself.

For several weeks he had been interviewing for one job after another, but somehow things just never seemed to click. On this particular day he was already running late for another interview when he spotted a woman stranded by her car with a flat tire.

What should he do? God's Word says do good to others and serve them regardless of the cost. But if he pulled off the road to help, he would completely miss his interview. Maybe he should just pass her by and shine God on. After all, God would understand. I mean, a guy's gotta be practical, right?

Still there were all those promises that God made, like this one in James that says if we do what God says, we'll be blessed.

It was a tough decision, but at the last minute he pulled over to help the stranded woman. He was already late and figured he might as well give God a shot at this blessing business.

Of course, by the time he was through and got the lady back on the road, there was no way he could keep the appointment. But he figured he'd drop by anyway, at least to apologize.

Imagine his surprise when he walked in, only to discover that the lady giving the interviews was the same one he had helped.

Guess who got the job?

God doesn't always hand us such neatly wrapped gifts. Things could have gone completely different. The guy could have shown up at the job interview and been tossed out for being so late. But that would have been OK too, because God would have had another job for him—a better one someplace else.

Jesus set the example for doing what God wanted. When Jesus agreed to obey the Father and go to the cross for us, it wasn't exactly a walk in the park for Him. He suffered all the pain and punishment that should have been ours. He endured all of God's wrath for our sins.

But when it was over, when all was said and done, He received—and continues to receive—as much glory, praise, and honor as God His Father.

I guess you could say that's being blessed.

All this to say: Hang in there. Keep doing good. Keep doing what God's Word says—even though at the time it doesn't make sense. Even though it may make you look like a total fool. Even though it seems to be the worst possible choice.

Because *eventually*, maybe not right away, but eventually, you will wind up being blessed.

ALWAYS.

PONDERING POINTS

☞ What ways have you seen God bless you or others for doing right (even when it seemed foolish)?

☞ Will He do it again?

From out of the Mouth

If anyone considers himself religious and yet does not keep a tight rein on his tongue, he deceives himself and his religion is worthless.
JAMES 1:26

Just as what you do is a good sign of what you believe, so is what you say. James is going to get to the tongue a little bit later. But right now the point he's making is this:

**If you say your mind's on heaven
but your mouth sounds like something from hell,
it's time for a little reevaluation.**

You may be thinking: "OK, OK, so what's wrong with a little 'damn' or 'hell' from time to time, just to spice things up, to help me fit in with my friends? After all, I don't want them thinking I'm a total loser. I mean, I'm not using God's name in vain or saying the big no-no words. They're just words, right?"

Right. But just as your actions should show that you're one of God's kids, so should your mouth.

What you say and how you say it is a sign to others stating:

"This is who I am. This is what I believe."

It's one of the ways the world labels and defines a person. God wants the world to know you are a Christian so He can use you (yes, even you) as a positive example. There's no better way than by watching what you say.

But James is talking about more than a little cussing now and then. He's also talking about put-downs.

If God is right (and He has that habit), then your mouth reveals what's actually in your heart.

For out of the overflow of the heart the mouth speaks.
Matthew 12:34

And if you're always putting people down, what does that really say about your concern and love for them?

I know, I know. Like everyone else, there are times I'd die for a good put-down line—especially when someone is giving me a hard time or being a total jerk.

And let's not forget how good put-downs are when you want to impress the group and show everyone how clever you are. They are great ways of gaining respect, great ways of feeling good about yourself.

But the point is that put-downs hurt. No matter how bright and clever, they're still putting someone down and making that person look stupid.

Why do we do it? So we can come off looking smart.

But putting someone down so we can look smart was not exactly what Jesus had in mind when He echoed the commandment, "love your neighbor."

Now that doesn't mean you have to go around complimenting everybody you see. And it doesn't mean you can't have a sense of humor. What Jesus minds is *meanness*…even a little.

So be sensitive about what you say and remember that every put-down hurts.

Try to say to others what you would want them to say to you. Words are important to God. Maybe that's why Jesus said:

I tell you that men will have to give account on the day of judgment for every careless word they have spoken. For by your words you will be acquitted [found innocent], and by your words you will be condemned.
Matthew 12:36,37

PONDERING POINTS

☞ Think of a time when you really put someone down. How did you feel?

☞ Think of a time when you were really put down. How did you feel?

☞ Did God feel any difference?

Real Religion

This is pure and undefiled religion in the sight of our God and Father, to visit orphans and widows in their distress.
JAMES 1:27 NASB

JESUS: Hi, Christian…well, don't just stand there, come on in. I can't tell you how good it is to see you. I've been waiting a long time for this moment.

CHRIS: Chris…

JESUS: Pardon Me?

CHRIS: My friends call me Chris.

JESUS: Oh, certainly…Chris.

CHRIS: Some place You got here.

JESUS: Thanks. Been preparing it a long time for you and the others—couple thousand years. Glad you like it.

CHRIS: Some of those mansions over on the east side—pretty impressive. I was wondering, which one of 'em is mine?

JESUS: Well, that's why you're here. Let's take a look at your record and see what We can give you.

CHRIS: Great! Guess You see in that book there that I never missed a Sunday—unless of course I'd been partying or there was a football game on the ol' tube.

JESUS: Hm-hm.

CHRIS: And sing—man alive, there wasn't a person in that congregation who could sing as loud as I did. And they all knew it too. You could tell by the way they winced that I loved to worship You. Really sang my heart out.

JESUS: Yes, I see…and that touched Me more than you can imagine, but tell Me—

CHRIS: And talk the talk—let me tell You, no one could rattle off Christianese like I could…"Well, praise the Lord, brother, I just gotta share with you how neat the good Lord is. How I was a sinner till I repented, accepted Him, and got saved by being washed in the blood of the Lamb. Glory!"

JESUS: That's all very impressive, Chris, but—

CHRIS: Must've spent a thousand dollars a year on all Your CDs—and don't forget the satellite dish we fixed up so we could catch and record all Your television shows on our new big screen TV…I mean, when we weren't serving you by "Jogging for Jesus" or playing on the church's "Bowling for Blessings" team.

JESUS: I see. Tell me, what about the widows and orphans?

CHRIS: The what?

JESUS: You know, all My children who were in such great need.

CHRIS: Never saw any.

JESUS: Did you look?

CHRIS: Never had time—I mean with the youth meetings, the car washes, the seminars, the retreats—and don't forget summer and winter camp. I mean, I was so busy serving You I never had a chance to…What's this?

JESUS: Your reward.

CHRIS: But…it looks like…Wait a minute, what am I supposed to do with a pup tent? Where's my mansion?

JESUS: Sorry, Chris, that's the best I could do with what you sent up. Could you send in the next person, please?

CHRIS: That little ragged African kid? Boy, is he in for a shock. I hear the believers in his village were so busy feeding the hungry they didn't even take time to build You a decent church. Tough break for him.

JESUS: I see your point—some people aren't into palaces. Hope the gardeners and servants I throw in will make it easier for him. Be seeing you around, Chris.

This is pure and undefiled religion in the sight of our God and Father, to visit orphans and widows in their distress.

PONDERING POINTS

☞ When's the last time you practiced "pure and undefiled religion"?

☞ What practical things can you do to practice more of it?

A Tough One

And to keep oneself unstained by the world.
JAMES 1:27 NASB

A whole book could be written on this command. And that's what it is—a command.

But how do you do it?

- How, when every time you turn on the tube or catch a flick there are a couple of perfect bods hopping in the sack?

- How, when the whole world screams, "Who cares about right and wrong! If it feels good, do it"?

- How, when purity and holiness are treated like jokes and everything that's wrong is twisted to look right?

How do you keep yourself "unstained"? It's not easy, but it's not impossible either.

The easiest and most obvious way is through avoidance. Stay away from R-rated movies and, yes, even some of the PG-13s. Ask around. Do a little research. Do they contain scenes that are unhealthy to see?

What about TV? The same thing. Be very, very selective. You've only got one soul. Why allow someone to get inside and dirty it up? If the show's no good, if it chips away at your beliefs in right and wrong, keep it off.

And what talk about the media would be complete without mentioning music? Ah, yes, the great battlefield. To listen or not to listen, that is the question. The point is, a lot of music (Christian and non) is good; and a lot is sewage. The decision whether to listen isn't always easy, but the guidelines should be something like these:

- Are the music and lyrics uplifting? Do they help you see life more clearly, enjoy it more deeply, understand how God would have you live it more fully? In other words, do they give to your life instead of trying to steal from it?

- Do they help you appreciate some aspect of our Creator or His creation? Do they stir up the joy, the peace, and the love He has surrounded you with? Or do they try to steal these gifts—replacing them with resentment, rebellion, desire, and lust?

The bottom line: Does the music draw you closer to the Lord and His goodness...or does it drag you into the world and its sickness?

Ah, come on. I watch and listen to that stuff all the time, and you don't see me doing drugs or becoming a sex maniac. That stuff doesn't really affect me.

Sorry, no sale.

According to experts across the country, there are few things that influence and shape our lives as much as the media. In fact, according to a study by J.L. Singer at Yale University...

"The outlook on any moral value can be changed through TV viewing."

Yeah, but lots of people are catching that film, watching that show, buying that CD.

That's true. And according to Jesus, lots of people are going to hell.

He was trying to let us know how He felt about this kind of purity when He said:

If your right eye causes you to sin, gouge it out and throw it away. It is better for you to lose one part of your body than for your whole body to be thrown into hell.
Matthew 5:29,30

Though this language is symbolic, He is asking for a significant sacrifice.

Yet how many of us won't even sacrifice a favorite show or recording artist? How many of us actually plop down hard-earned cash to expose ourselves to the very sins God warns us to avoid?

It's true that there are things that people of the world do that we should not. Things they listen to that we shouldn't. Places they go that we mustn't. But then again, we'll eventually be doing things, listening to things, and going places they can't even begin to imagine.

We are a special people—people set aside for God and His love. We must treat ourselves with that respect and care.

**If we're Christians, we're unique, priceless.
And our calling is far different, far higher
than the rest of the world's.**

We are royalty. And God demands that we treat ourselves as such.

PONDERING POINTS

☞ Are you seeing any movies or shows that God doesn't want you to see?

☞ Do you have CDs He doesn't want you to have?

☞ What are you going to do about them?

5
WHO'S IMPORTANT?

Discrimination

My brothers, as believers in our glorious Lord Jesus Christ, don't show favoritism. Suppose a man comes into your meeting wearing a gold ring and fine clothes, and a poor man in shabby clothes also comes in. If you show special attention to the man wearing fine clothes and say, "Here's a good seat for you," but say to the poor man, "You stand there," or "Sit on the floor by my feet," have you not discriminated among yourselves and become judges with evil thoughts?
JAMES 2:1-4

If you were a multibillionaire and one guy came up to you with 20 cents and another came up with five cents, would you look upon the first guy as a whole lot richer than the second?

Or if the entire universe loved and worshiped you, would you look upon a person with 20 friends as being super popular?

Probably not.

The same is true with God. He's got everything He could ever want. He's not impressed by wealth, popularity, fame, or even talent.

And we shouldn't be either.

But almost against our will we find ourselves being pulled in that direction. Oh, we may pretend it doesn't affect us, but don't we pay just a little bit more attention to Superjock with the Jaguar? Don't we pay just a little more attention to Superbod with all the right curves in all the right places?

Or what about spending our time with the popular "in" group while avoiding contact with the shy or lonely loser?

Of course we do it—everybody does. It's only natural.

But, once again James is telling us to:

Be supernatural.

If we're heirs to all that God has—including His fame, popularity, and fortune—why should we be impressed by what little others have? Nobody's fortune will rival ours; nobody's fame will come close to ours; nobody's popularity will be as great as ours. After all, we're going to be sitting with the King of the universe!

But we keep buying Satan's lies—that we're a nobody, just another number, not very special, not very important. So we feel we have to hang with people who are important—hoping that we can somehow enjoy *their* importance or make other people think we share in it.

If we could just believe the fact that we are important, that because Jesus bought us with a terribly high price— His life—He now considers us incredibly precious.

If we could just understand how invaluable He has made us, then we would have no need to pay special attention to the "special" people...hoping they show us a special favor, or hoping that others think we are special.

WE *ARE* SPECIAL—THE MOST SPECIAL PEOPLE IN THE UNIVERSE!

And if we really began to understand that, if that really became a part of our lives, then we could begin to look on everybody equally.

We would truly begin to see that the poor, the disadvantaged, the losers are just as important as the rich, the popular, the famous.

We would begin to see them all through God's eyes, as people in desperate need of His love.

PONDERING POINTS

☞ Can you think of a couple of losers in your school?

☞ Consider making an effort to reach out to them. You don't have to become best friends, but make a point to let them know you consider them a part of the human race.

God and the Poor

Listen, my dear brothers: Has not God chosen those who are poor in the eyes of the world to be rich in faith and to inherit the kingdom he promised those who love him? But you have insulted the poor. Is it not the rich who are exploiting you? Are they not the ones who are dragging you into court? Are they not the ones who are slandering the noble name of him to whom you belong?
JAMES 2:5-7

God has a special place in His heart for the poor. In fact, one of the proofs Jesus used to convince John the Baptist that He is the Christ was that He preached the gospel to the poor. And let's not forget the Sermon on the Mount, when He said: "Blessed are you who are poor, for yours is the kingdom of God" (Luke 6:20).

But *why?*

Why are the poor so important to God?

One reason is that they are the despised, the downtrodden, the ones rejected by everybody else. And because God is into love and comfort, what better people to reach out to than those who need it most?

Another important reason is that the poor know they need help. It doesn't take much to convince the poor that they need God to work in their lives, to help meet their needs, to save their souls. The rich, on the other hand, think they can buy whatever they need and don't really see any use for God.

I have the chance to work with youth around the world, and I've got to tell you the toughest places to get kids to fall in love with Jesus are the wealthy places. After all, if Mommy and Daddy can buy them whatever they want, what do they need God for?

But the poor, they are the ones whose hands reach out to God. And because God loves to fill hands, they are the ones who get blessed. Of course, the same is true for the rich, if they humble themselves and reach out to God.

James really wants us to understand this:

God has a special place for the poor in His heart, and if we want to be in on God's plan, then it would be smart to treat them like He wants us to.

But a lot of times we don't. We treat them like the rest of the world treats them, saving our partiality for the rich.

But James explains that it's usually the rich who scoff at Christianity. They are the ones who tend to break Christ's commands, who refuse to love their fellowman as themselves. They are the ones inclined to step on others, who bend the rules so they can stay rich, who drag people into court so they can keep or get more money.

Yet it is the rich we find ourselves wanting to chum around with and buddy up to the most.

Strange…

Well, once again God wants to change our strangeness. Once again He wants us to stop thinking like the world and start thinking like Him.

PONDERING POINTS

☞ Can you think of times you've ignored the poor?

☞ What are some ways you can reach out to the down-trodden?

God Doesn't Grade on a Curve

If, however, you are fulfilling the royal law, according to the Scripture, "YOU SHALL LOVE YOUR NEIGHBOR AS YOURSELF," you are doing well. But if you show partiality, you are committing sin and are convicted by the law as transgressors. For whoever keeps the whole law and yet stumbles in one point, he has become guilty of all. For He who said, "DO NOT COMMIT ADULTERY," also said, "DO NOT COMMIT MURDER." Now if you do not commit adultery, but do commit murder, you have become a transgressor of the law.
JAMES 2:8-11 NASB

Jim-Bob is finally ready for his big date. He has done everything right to impress the girl. He found out her favorite restaurant, rented a limo, even rented a velvet, *all-white* tuxedo! (This may seem a little extravagant but, then again, you don't know Jim-Bob. He needs all the help he can get.)

Anyway, so he's heading out the door past his family, who are already eating dinner, when Mom insists on giving him the ol' goodbye kiss.

No problem.

The problem comes when cute little Mary Beth reaches out and grabs his white lapel with her cute little two-year-old hand...*that's dripping in spaghetti sauce!*

The tux is ruined!

So is Jim-Bob's date. It's only a little red smear, but there's no way he can wear that tux now.

The same is true with us. A little sin can ruin us. Just one little sin makes us guilty of breaking the whole law.

Jim-Bob can't go out on his date and say, "I know there's a bright red stain on the front, but look at the rest of the tux—I mean, the rest of it is white."

And we won't be able to stand before God and say, "I know I have a little sin (that I never confessed or wanted to get fixed up), but look at the rest of me. I mean, the rest of me is clean."

That's the point James is trying to make.

**God does not grade on a curve.
He wants us *completely* whole, not partially whole.**

Jesus wants to heal us and make us secure enough in His love so that we, in turn, will be able to reach out and love our neighbors as ourselves.

But if we love only our rich neighbor, or popular neighbor, or the neighbor who can do us the most good, then we're in trouble. We're only fulfilling part of the law. And fulfilling only part of God's command is as good as fulfilling none of it.

**That doesn't mean we live in trembling neurosis
because we're not fulfilling all of God's Word.
But we have to confess that we're not cutting it
and allow Him to help change us.**

And eventually we should be able to reach out to the unlovely, the embarrassing, the poor. Eventually, we should be able to lay down our reputations and befriend the unpopular, the unlovable—trusting that God will somehow give us His love for them.

It's not always easy. But it's not all that hard either... once you step out. All you have to do is be willing and make the initial effort.

It's up to God to do the rest.

Consider what Scripture says about those who reach out to others and those who don't:

Then the King will say to those on his right, "Come, you who are blessed by my Father, take your inheritance, the kingdom prepared for you since the creation of the world. For I was hungry and you gave me something to eat, I was thirsty and you gave me something to drink, I was a stranger and you invited me in, I needed clothes and you clothed me, I was sick and you looked after me, I was in prison and you came to visit me."

Then the righteous will answer him, "Lord, when did we see you hungry and feed you, or thirsty and give you something to drink? When did we see you a stranger and invite you in, or needing clothes and clothe you? When did we see you sick or in prison and go to visit you?"

The King will reply, "I tell you the truth, *whatever you did for one of the least of these brothers of mine, you did for me.*"
Matthew 25:34-40

A pretty radical concept, but one God takes pretty seriously.

You see, being right with God is more than just saying the magic words and becoming a Christian. It's even more than allowing Him to make you pure and holy...

It's also taking the love that He's poured into your heart and pouring it into others.

PONDERING POINTS

☞ What are the little sins you think you "can get away"
with?

☞ What are some better ways you can "love your neighbor
as yourself"?

The Law of Liberty

Speak and act as those who are going to be judged by the law that gives freedom, because judgment without mercy will be shown to anyone who has not been merciful. Mercy triumphs over judgment!
JAMES 2:12,13

Once again, after making it clear what's right and what's wrong, James tells us to go out and do it—to "speak and act" accordingly.

The book of James does a lot of this, and that's good. So many people like the book because it gives them practical, hands-on advice about what to do and what not to do.

But to some of us it can become a trap, an endless list of do's and don'ts, a heavy burden that we start carrying around. It drives us deeper and deeper into guilt and hopelessness because we're sure we'll never be able to please God.

In fact, one heavy-duty theologian in the sixteenth century (Martin Luther) wanted to throw it out of the Bible altogether! Seems he felt James mentioned a few too many times that we have to live by the law (as opposed to the grace of Jesus Christ).

But James is talking about an entirely different law—the law of *liberty*.

It's true we'll never be able to work our way to heaven. We'll never be accepted by God because we're so perfect—because we've done everything we're supposed to do and refused everything we're not supposed to. No way.

That's why we need Jesus. Because we are going to mess up. Repeat after me: *I am going to mess up.* But... you don't have to.

You can be free from messing up.
That's what the law of liberty is all about.

Say what?

Before we became Christians we were slaves to sin. We were actually controlled by the world's lusts, its desires, its ME FIRST mentality. We couldn't help ourselves. Oh, we may have done something nice for somebody from time to time, but it was generally so we could get something good in return—even if it meant just feeling good for being so good!

But when we received Christ and asked Him to live inside our hearts—to actually live there—He broke the power that was controlling us. He freed us. Now we have the desire and ability to really start caring for others and for the Lord.

That's what Christianity is all about.

Christianity is not a bunch of dusty rules and regulations
that we have to follow or feel terribly guilty about
not following...it's *a relationship*.

A relationship with God.

And once we have that relationship, He starts empowering us to do good—not because we *have* to but because we *want* to!

It's like me doing things for my wife. I empty the cat box not because I have to, not because it's in my marriage contract, but because I want to (well, sort of). Because I know it makes her happy. Even when the couch potato part of me doesn't want to help, the loving husband part of me does. And that's the part I listen to.

It's the same as with us and God. Once our hearts become born again we start doing good things not because we have to, but because we want to.

There's a big difference.

One is an old heart that tries to do good but constantly fails. The other is a new, God-given heart that starts to do good naturally, because that's its nature.

PONDERING POINTS

☞ What areas of sin is God freeing you from?

☞ What areas haven't you let Him touch?

6
FAITH THAT WORKS

The Real Deal

What good is it, my brothers, if a man claims to have faith but has no deeds? Can such faith save him? Suppose a brother or sister is without clothes and daily food. If one of you says to him, "Go, I wish you well; keep warm and well fed," but does nothing about his physical needs, what good is it? In the same way, faith by itself, if it is not accompanied by action, is dead.
JAMES 2:14-17

Many people think becoming a Christian is like joining a new club. Once they say the magic words (asking Jesus to forgive them and live inside their hearts), they've been through the initiation and now they just sit back and coast to heaven. After all, we're saved by faith in Jesus Christ—in what He did for us on the cross—and not our own works. Right?

Right.

That's the first step. But what do we do after that? Just sit around and have a good time while the rest of the world is literally going to hell?

Somehow, I get the feeling that isn't quite what God has in mind.

If a person becomes a lifeguard and someone begins to drown, does he simply shout, "You'll be OK. I'm a lifeguard!" and then lean back in his chair to catch a few more rays while the person drowns? Of course not. He gets in there and helps. That's why he's a lifeguard. That's the whole reason he's been trained and given the power to save lives—so he can save lives.

Yet how many Christians, when they see somebody in desperate need, say, "You'll be OK. I've got faith that somehow you'll get something to eat," and then head to the mall to buy the latest wardrobe?

Faith without the works to back it up is useless.

James says it's "dead." In fact, he says that if you claim you have faith in Jesus but never put that faith into action, there's a good chance you are *not* saved!

You cannot separate faith and works. They go hand in hand. First comes the faith—which, in turn, gives you the power to do the works. You cannot have one without the other.

If you say you have the faith but don't have the accompanying works, chances are you've got the *wrong type faith*. Christ-given faith does both. It believes *and* does.

This may have been one of Jesus' points when He told John to deliver a sobering message to a group of believers in Laodicea:

**I know your deeds [works], that you are neither cold
nor hot. I wish you were either one or the other!
So, because you are lukewarm—neither hot
nor cold—I am about to spit you out of my mouth.**
Revelation 3:15,16

PONDERING POINTS

☞ What areas of your deeds are on fire with God?

☞ What areas are cold or just lukewarm?

Good Fruit

But someone will say, "You have faith; I have deeds." Show me your faith without deeds, and I will show you my faith by what I do. You believe that there is one God. Good! Even the demons believe that—and shudder.
JAMES 2:18,19

Anticipating an argument over his insistence that we be doers and not just hearers, James takes the other person's side for just a minute:

"What's the big deal, Jimmy? Why are you making all the fuss? So I happen to be into faith, and you happen to be into works. I believe that God is going to save me regardless of what I do, and you think we should serve Him. The important thing is that we both believe, right? I mean, that's all that counts…that we believe."

But James' answer is quick and to the point: "You believe? Well whoop-de-do, that's very good, we're all impressed. But there's one little problem…*so do demons.* And they're not exactly going to make it to heaven."

You don't have to be smart to believe in God. You don't even have to be good. I mean, let's face it, Satan and his demons never won any good-guy awards.

But to actually have Jesus inside controlling the shots—to obey Him, to let Him be the boss, to let Him be your Lord—well now, that's a little different.

And as you obey Him and let Him run the show, He'll tell you when it's time to reach out to someone in need. It just comes naturally.

You don't have to go around sweating it, wondering if you're doing enough good works to squeeze into heaven. Forget that. Heaven's a free gift because of what Jesus did for us on the cross. There's nothing you can do to earn it.

But once you're saved, it's up to you to use that power and love He's given you to reach out and help others. And that's not something you have to get tied up in knots about. The works will come naturally. If you have faith in Jesus Christ and allow Him to be the boss of your life, then the good works will come—just as naturally as fruit appears on a fruit tree.

Do you ever go outside and hear apple trees grunting and groaning to grow fruit? Of course not. That's how they're made. Growing apples just comes naturally to apple trees.

The same is true with us. As people in love with God, doing good works just comes naturally.

All we have to do is be willing. Jesus does the rest.

Perhaps He put it best when He said:

By their fruit you will recognize them. Do people pick grapes from thornbushes, or figs from thistles? Likewise every good tree bears good fruit, but a bad tree bears bad fruit. A good tree cannot bear bad fruit, and a bad tree cannot bear good fruit. Every tree that does not bear good fruit is cut down and thrown into the fire. Thus, by their fruit you will recognize them.
Matthew 7:16-20

He goes on to finish with a sobering note to those who say they believe, but don't act like it:

Not everyone who says to me, "Lord, Lord," will enter the kingdom of heaven, but *only he who does the will* of my *Father* who is in heaven. *Many* will say to me on that day, "Lord, Lord, did we not prophesy in your name, and in your name drive out demons and perform many miracles?" Then I will tell them plainly, I never knew you. Away from me, you evildoers!

Matthew 7:21-23

PONDERING POINTS

☞ What areas are you talking the God talk but not walking the God walk?

☞ Will you allow God to fix them?

Complete Faith

You foolish man, do you want evidence that faith without deeds is useless? Was not our ancestor Abraham considered righteous for what he did when he offered his son Isaac on the altar? You see that his faith and his actions were working together, and his faith was made complete by what he did. And the scripture was fulfilled that says, "Abraham believed God, and it was credited to him as righteousness," and he was called God's friend. You see that a person is justified by what he does and not by faith alone.
JAMES 2:20-24

James figures this whole idea of faith *and* works isn't going to be that easy for some to swallow, so he gives a couple examples using some Old Testament heroes.

First there was Abraham—the very father of the Jewish nation. As you recall, he and his wife Sarah waited for years and years to have a kid. Then, when all appeared hopeless, when Sarah was far too old to possibly have a child, surprise! It's stork time. At last, Abraham had a son. Finally he could start populating the earth with his descendants just as God had promised so many years before. All of his hopes and dreams, all of God's promises, rested in this one little child. Needless to say, Abraham was thrilled.

But a few years later God had another little surprise: He asked Abraham to kill the boy!

Talk about being in a hard place. Abraham knew God loved him and wouldn't break His promise about making

101

him the father of many nations. Yet God was now asking him to kill his son and destroy the only hope of that promise ever coming true.

But in faith Abraham went to the mountaintop, built an altar, and prepared to kill his son.

His faith was not a matter of just saying, "God, I believe You love me and will keep Your promises. So let's just call the whole thing off, OK? I mean, I believe, so that's good enough."

Instead, his faith consisted of both believing *and* obeying.

He tied up his son, laid him on the altar, raised his knife to kill him—and then, at the last second when God was absolutely certain Abraham would go through with it, He stopped him.

It was a hard test, but Abraham passed. He had real faith—faith that consisted of both believing and doing. In fact, as James says, it was the "doing" that made his faith complete.

And it was this type of *complete* faith that made Abraham righteous before God, that makes us righteous before Him, and that allows both Abraham and us to be called "God's friends."

PONDERING POINTS

☞ In what areas has God tested your faith?

☞ Did you pull through for Him?

☞ Did He pull through for you?

☞ Did He do it right away?

Faith Without Works Is Dead

In the same way, was not even Rahab the prostitute considered righteous for what she did when she gave lodging to the spies and sent them off in a different direction? As the body without the spirit is dead, so faith without deeds is dead.
JAMES 2:25,26

James gives one more example that faith is about both believing and doing. Back in the book of Joshua, when Israel was getting ready to enter the Promised Land, they sent some spies into Jericho to find out what was happening.

Things got a little tense for them there, and they wound up having to hide on a prostitute's rooftop. The prostitute's name was Rahab.

During the discussion up there she made it quite clear that she believed God was who He said He was: "For the LORD your God is God in heaven above and on the earth below" (Joshua 2:11). She also believed that the Israelites would capture her city, just as God had promised.

But simply believing all this was not enough. Because she believed, she also acted by helping the spies escape. And as a result of this type of faith—*believing and doing*—when the Israelites finally took the town, her life was spared.

Not only was she spared, but she is mentioned in the Bible several times because of her faith. In fact, God gave her the privilege of becoming an ancestor directly related to Jesus Christ! No small honor.

**All because she had the right type of faith.
A faith that didn't just believe—but a faith
that put its belief into action.**

This is true faith. This is *complete* faith. For faith without the doing is really no faith at all. Faith without the doing is dead and useless.

PONDERING POINTS

☞ What areas of your life prove your faith is alive?

☞ Where does your "doing" need to be stronger?

7
WORDS THAT BURN

On Teaching

Not many of you should presume to be teachers, my brothers, because you know that we who teach will be judged more strictly.
JAMES 3:1

Nearly everyone likes to be in charge. "Do this. Do that. Do it my way."

Being the boss, the one running the show, makes you feel important.

But James warns us to be careful, especially when it comes to teaching about spiritual matters. Why? A couple of reasons.

First, no topic is more important than a person's relationship with God.

If you teach somebody the wrong principles in mathematics, he'll probably mess up his SAT or become the world's worst accountant, but he'll still get by. If you teach someone gibberish and tell him it's Spanish, he'll feel pretty stupid when he visits Mexico, but he'll survive.

But if you teach him the wrong principles about loving and serving God and he believes you, then you've fouled up his entire life.

Second, teachers will be judged more strictly. If you go around telling people right from wrong but don't do right yourself, there's no way you can stand before God and say, "Hey, give me a break. I didn't know."

All *this* is to say:

Teaching people about God is serious business and not something to be taken lightly.

That doesn't mean you go around shaking in your boots, afraid to tell anybody about Jesus or what He's done in your life. On the contrary, He *wants* you to tell people about Him. And don't worry about messing up, 'cause He'll always be there to help. I mean, it's His reputation that's on the line, right? He's not going to let you botch it too badly.

All James is saying is let's make certain that we're really called to be teachers (and the Bible says some of us are). But if we're not, let's not go around trying to run the show or pretending we have all the answers.

PONDERING POINTS

☞ What's the most rewarding thing about teaching some-body?

☞ Imagine what that feels like when the subject happens to be eternal.

Me and My Big Mouth

*We all stumble in many ways. If anyone is never at fault
in what he says, he is a perfect man, able to keep his whole
body in check. When we put bits into the mouths of horses
to make them obey us, we can turn the whole animal. Or take
ships as an example. Although they are so large and are driven
by strong winds, they are steered by a very small rudder
wherever the pilot wants to go. Likewise the tongue is a small
part of the body, but it makes great boasts. Consider what
a great forest is set on fire by a small spark. The tongue also is
a fire, a world of evil among the parts of the body. It corrupts
the whole person, sets the whole course of his life on fire, and
is itself set on fire by hell.*
JAMES 3:2-6

James has a lot to say here, so let's take it a bit at a time.

1. We all mess up.

Not only do we all mess up, but James says we all mess up
in *"many ways."* That should be encouraging when you
get to thinking you're some sort of spiritual reject, or that
you're the only one sinning. We all sin. Our goal is to get
better and sin less. But getting better can sometimes be a
painfully slow process.

DON'T GET DISCOURAGED WITH YOURSELF.

God won't give up on you. He's going to be right there
at your side, working right along with you until together

the two of you can overcome the problem areas. (And with God on your team, what are the chances of losing?)

2. One of the most common ways of sinning is with your mouth.

We've talked a little bit about this before. The tongue is one of the quickest ways of seeing what's really in a person's heart. And if what's inside is garbage, it won't be too long before garbage starts rolling out of the mouth.

3. As you learn to control your tongue, you can control yourself.

Control of your tongue can, to a certain extent, control the direction of your life, just as a bit in a horse's mouth controls the entire animal. The same is true with ships controlled by a rudder. No matter how strong the wind is or how big the boat is, the pilot will be able to steer in the direction he wants to go if he has control of the rudder. You will steer in the direction you want to go if you control your tongue.

4. The tongue does all the bragging.

Even though it's one of the smallest parts of the body, it makes great boasts.

5. The tongue is like a tiny spark in a dry forest.

It doesn't seem like much but suddenly, before you know it, things get out of hand and that spark sets the entire forest on fire. It gets you doing things you know you really shouldn't be doing, treating people the way they really shouldn't be treated. When misused, the tongue can set your entire life on fire—destroying your dreams and your hopes, ruining other people's lives, causing incredible pain to those you love.

It's a pretty deadly weapon.

And who is trying to destroy your life with that fire? Who is constantly trying to get your tongue to run out of control? According to James, there's only one source of all this temptation: the pit of hell.

And, as we've said before, there's only one way to beat hell...

PONDERING POINTS

☞ Got a problem with your mouth?

☞ Does God want you to solve it?

☞ How?

Only One Way

All kinds of animals, birds, reptiles and creatures of the sea are being tamed and have been tamed by man, but no man can tame the tongue. It is a restless evil, full of deadly poison. With the tongue we praise our Lord and Father, and with it we curse men, who have been made in God's likeness. Out of the same mouth come praise and cursing. My brothers, this should not be. Can both fresh water and salt water flow from the same spring? My brothers, can a fig tree bear olives, or a grapevine bear figs? Neither can a salt spring produce fresh water.
JAMES 3:7-12

Bertha was a good person. She had her act pretty well together with the Lord, put other people before herself, and had even been known to pass on TV from time to time to read her Bible. I mean, we're talking radical Christianity here.

There was only one problem.

Bertha had a big mouth.

Seemed like she was always talking about somebody behind his back—gossiping, or using that quick wit of hers to slice people into little pieces. It wasn't something she did on purpose. It just seemed like the words jumped out of her mouth before she could catch them.

Finally it was time for drastic action.

No longer would she be the cause of ruined reputations. No longer would she pass along negative comments about somebody else. No longer would she embarrass someone or hurt his feelings with some clever, pithy saying. Bertha had found a cure.

But it wasn't too long before her fiancé started complaining. I mean, kissing a mouth covered with masking tape was not his idea of a great time.

Next came the superglue. A good idea, except when it came to eating.

Finally there was the surgery. With lips permanently sealed she could at last be at peace. Never again would she cut down somebody. Never again would she pass on damaging information. Never again would she sin. At last Bertha was free...until someone made the mistake of teaching her sign language.

The point is:

**We cannot control the mouth—
we cannot tame the tongue.**

It's absolutely impossible.

We have to go deeper, to the root cause, to the real problem—the heart. That's where the bad thoughts come from. That's the contaminated spring where the water begins. If it can be cleaned up, then we'd have no problem with what flowed out of our mouths.

And as we dwell with Jesus, as we allow Him to get into our hearts and clean things up, that's exactly what happens; our speech starts to change. Not because we're forcing it, but because it just happens naturally. As naturally as a tree with healthy roots bears good fruit.

He's doing the cultivating and growing and harvesting, not us.

All we have to do is be willing to let Him.

Now it's true, there will be times when we feel discouraged, full of guilt, hopeless. "O Lord, I've done it again."

But hang in there. He's on our side. And, if we keep letting Him have His way, eventually those thorns and briars we are currently bearing will be transformed to fruit—a fruit that is a help, a joy, and a pleasure to all who eat of it. Don't ask me how. It's just another one of those "God things."

PONDERING POINTS

☞ Where have you seen God clean up your speech?

☞ Where have you turned down His help?

☞ What's the key to letting Him?

8
WISE UP

The Real Leaders

*Who is wise and understanding among you? Let him show it
by his good life, by deeds done in the humility that comes
from wisdom.*
JAMES 3:13

The world is full of wanna-be leaders. People want
power so badly they'll say anything to convince us that
they're the ones with all the wisdom and experience.

James' point is simple:

**Put your life where your mouth is.
Show us, don't tell us.**

Real leaders, the ones who have had the greatest effect
on our world, are usually not kings, governors, or presi-
dents—not even Hollywood heartthrobs. History has
proven that those who have had the greatest effect on the
world are those who quietly go about their day-to-day

work, never drawing attention to themselves, never dreaming of glory.

Like that old-timer who had been herding livestock out in the sticks some 40 years until he had a little run-in with a burning bush. And even then he kept arguing with God, telling Him He had the wrong man. No way could Moses see himself leading all those Jewish folks to the Promised Land and becoming one of the greatest leaders ever to live on the face of the earth.

Or what about that Carpenter who was born in a barn, grew up in a backwoods village, lived off the donations of His followers, and died on a cross in some obscure country? You might say Jesus had a bit of an effect on this old planet.

These are the types of people who shake the world. Not the politicians, not the rocket scientists, not the rock stars; but those who quietly and humbly go about their day-to-day business—they are the real leaders.

My favorite movie of all time is an oldie called *It's a Wonderful Life*. It's a story of a nothing man in a nothing business who keeps dreaming of getting out of his nothing town to become *somebody*. But every time he gets his chance, someone needs his help and he stays behind to give a hand. It's never anything earthshaking. He just helps them out with the little things he is able to do.

Well, time goes on. His old buddy becomes a business tycoon and his brother becomes a war hero. It seems everybody keeps becoming somebody—except him. He just keeps staying behind doing the little things for those who need his help. One thing leads to another and, eventually, he becomes so discouraged over how "worthless" his life is that he tries to kill himself.

It is then that an angel suddenly appears, takes him by the hand, and shows him what the world would have been like if he had never lived. Through dramatic illustrations he makes it clear how those tiny, unnoticed acts of love had actually changed and revolutionized his entire community—how one person's life, though lived unnoticed, can influence the outcome of thousands, even millions of other lives.

This is what James is talking about.

Keep doing the little, unnoticed acts of self-sacrifice and love. You may never make the headlines. You may never star in a music video. In fact, you may never get any recognition—at least this side of heaven.

But every moment is being recorded and will be used in that great celebration on the other side.

And, even more important, every moment will have a positive effect on the rest of the world. Let me repeat that:

Every moment lived in quiet obedience to God will have a positive effect on our world.

Those moments may seem insignificant. They may not seem too profound. But they will always change our world for the better.

Always.

PONDERING POINTS

☞ Who was the seventeenth president of the United States?

☞ Who won the Academy Award for best actor three years ago?

☞ Don't know? Here's another one—name two or three people who have been a positive influence on your life. Will you ever forget what they did for you?

☞ Will God?

☞ Why not?

Wisdom from Hell

But if you have bitter jealousy and selfish ambition in your heart, do not be arrogant and so lie against the truth. This wisdom is not that which comes down from above, but is earthly, natural, demonic. For where jealousy and selfish ambition exist, there is disorder and every evil thing.
JAMES 3:14-16 NASB

There are two types of wisdom in this world—one from heaven, the other from hell. And they are constantly at war with one another, both in the world and in our own minds.

We've just looked into the wisdom that comes from heaven, but let's take a moment to look at the wisdom from hell. *It's jealous.* It's always looking at the other person, always comparing.

- It's not fair. Why wasn't I chosen? I'm just as good as she is.

- How come the good things always happen to him?

- Why does she look like someone off the cover of *Seventeen* while I belong on the cover of *Popular Mechanics?*

Have these thoughts ever run through your mind? Chances are they have. So congratulations; you've experienced jealousy! You've experienced hellish wisdom.

Before you go out and beat yourself with a whip, remember, we've *all* had those thoughts. The trick is simply to recognize their source and refuse to let them take root.

Jealousy, like so many other sins, boils down to not trusting God, not believing how much He really loves us.

Each person is unique. You're custom made. There isn't another one exactly like you in the entire universe. So God has a special way of working with and blessing each one of us.

It would be foolish if I sulked because my brother got a new pair of size 12 shoes and all I got were 10s. I mean, they're both new pairs of shoes and they both fit perfectly; they're just custom made for our uniqueness.

We're each specially built, specially unique. We're individually loved by God, and He works with us and loves us on an individual basis.

When you understand that, when you really begin to take hold of that truth, then you'll have no need to look at other people and compare. You'll know that they're getting the very best for them, and you're getting the very best for you.

When you understand how much God loves you, jealousy will make a fast exit.

Another sign of wisdom from hell is selfish ambition. It comes up in ideas like these:

- Are you really getting your fair share?

- If you don't look out for number one, no one else will.

- What do you get out of it?

Sound familiar? It should. The world is full of this type of self-centered thinking, and it's tough to stop it from invading our minds.

But it still comes from hell. It still tells us God is not going to provide. That we can't trust Him. That we have to go out there and do it ourselves. That we must put ourselves before others, before serving God.

Yet the Lord tells us over and over and over again that if we put others first, if we serve Him our lives will be unbelievably full, filled to maximum capacity with joy.

It may not mean you'll be making megabucks, buying a Porsche or living in a fancy mansion. But it will mean that you'll have the joy, peace, and love that the people buying those things are trying to find through those things.

And you'll also have the added comfort of knowing that He'll always provide for your every need.

Always.

> **So do not worry, saying, "What shall we eat?" or "What shall we drink?" or "What shall we wear?" For the pagans run after all these things, and your heavenly Father knows that you need them. But seek first his kingdom and his righteousness, and all these things will be given to you as well.**
> Matthew 6:31-33

There are two keys to fighting off wisdom from hell as it tries to invade your mind.

First, recognize its source and try to refuse it.

Second, if it keeps nagging, concentrate on remembering how much God really loves you. Dwell on that love by praising and thanking Him. There's something incredibly powerful about praise—something supernatural. I'm not sure what it is, but through praise I've seen impossible situations change. Even when I didn't feel like it and literally had to force myself, I have praised and thanked God and then seen Him work out impossible situations to His glory.

Some of this power exists because God actually lives within the praises of His people (Psalm 22:3 KJV). Some of it is present because we're joining in with what the rest of the universe does 24/7.

I'm not sure of all the whys. All I know is that by obeying Scripture, "always giving thanks to God the Father for everything" (Ephesians 5:20), I release a type of faith that allows God to work miraculously through every problem and impossibility.

God's overpowering love for us will always prevail. It will always provide. He has paid too great a price to forget about us or to give us anything but His very best. Hang on to that regardless of how foolish His wisdom may appear at times. Hang on to that when you don't understand right away what God is doing in a situation. Because…

Hellish wisdom will eventually burn. But heavenly wisdom will always prevail.

PONDERING POINTS

☞ What are a couple big things you feel jealous about?

☞ Have you confessed those feelings to God? (Remember, He's on your side.)

☞ The next time jealousy arises, try smashing it down with praise.

More on Heavenly Wisdom

But the wisdom from above is first pure, then peaceable, gentle, reasonable, full of mercy and good fruits, unwavering, without hypocrisy. And the seed whose fruit is righteousness is sown in peace by those who make peace.
JAMES 3:17,18 NASB

Heavenly wisdom is like cream. No matter how rough and tumble the situation, it will always rise to the top. It doesn't scream, argue, or fight to get there; but somehow, almost unnoticeably, it rises to the surface of the situation.

Let's look at some of the other attributes of heavenly wisdom:

1. It's pure.

As we allow God's heavenly wisdom to invade our lives, it enables us to think and see and live more purely. Our choices become more godly, more like ones Jesus would make.

2. It's peaceable.

Remember, your battle is never against people. They're not the enemy, they're the victims of the enemy. They're the ones you're trying to help. If someone's giving you a hard time, heavenly wisdom encourages you not to fight back with the weapons they're using—their mouths, their fists, their guns, their lawyers. It directs you to go to your spiritual arsenal and fight them with God's weapons—prayer, kindness, and love.

And don't pray that God will "wipe them out" or secretly look forward to judgment day when "God'll show 'em." Pray that He will forgive them and take the darkness from their eyes now, before it's too late.

3. It's gentle.

Heavenly wisdom encourages you not to fight and fret so things go your way. Forget the hysterical routine. If you've prayed about a situation, then you can rest assured that God will take care of it, however *He* sees fit. Even if it's not your way, you know it will be for the best.

4. It's reasonable.

Heavenly wisdom helps you to be flexible. Don't insist things always be done such and such a way. Look around you. God's pretty creative. Sometimes He likes to do the same thing but in an entirely different way. Stay open. And if someone's "new way" doesn't compromise your faith, give it a try. It just might be better.

5. It's full of mercy.

Heavenly wisdom reminds us not to hold grudges. Since God has forgiven us of so much, who are we to hold grudges against others? Besides, if we've ever said the Lord's Prayer, "Forgive us our debts, as we also have forgiven our debtors" (Matthew 6:12), and there are people we're still not forgiving, we may be in for some bad news.

6. It's full of good fruits.

Heavenly wisdom encourages you to say and do good things not because you strain and work at it, but because it comes naturally—as naturally as a good tree bears good fruit.

7. It's unwavering.

Heavenly wisdom encourages you to *continue* following God and doing good. As the storms of life whip people all about and you stand firm, you'll find people eventually turning to you for support—and as a result some may even turn to Jesus.

8. It's without hypocrisy.

Heavenly wisdom teaches us not to fake it, but to live it.

That's quite a list. As you pay attention to heavenly wisdom every one of these areas will take root in your life and grow. All you have to do is stay close to Jesus. All you have to do is let the Gardener do His job and care for you. The fruit will come. Just rest in Him.

PONDERING POINTS

☞ When's the last time you've seen a fruit tree stress and strain to bear its fruit?

☞ What's your responsibility in bearing fruit?

☞ What's God's?

9

ONE OR THE OTHER

Why War?

What causes fights and quarrels among you? Don't they come from your desires that battle within you? You want something but don't get it. You kill and covet, but you cannot have what you want. You quarrel and fight. You do not have, because you do not ask God.
JAMES **4:1,2**

Every battle, every war that has ever been fought, comes down to one reason: somebody wants something. Napoleon wanted Europe. North Vietnam and friends wanted South Vietnam. Hitler wanted the world.

With the cause that obvious, then the solution for world peace should be simple: convince people to be content with what they have.

Right. And while we're at it, let's try to stop the earth from revolving around the sun.

Because people don't believe God is looking out for their best interests, because of the "hellish wisdom" that says, "Look out for number one, you won't have enough, you must take in order to get," we will always have war. It's human nature.

But once again, James is encouraging us to be super-human, to allow Jesus to help us get rid of those fears and selfish desires and give us the courage and *faith* to put the other guy first. It's possible.

The only problem is, many aren't doing that. I mean, look at all the fighting and backbiting that goes on even between Christians. And the reason is just the same.

**We don't really believe God is in control.
We feel we have to look out for our own interests.**

We forget all about putting the other guy first. We forget all about prayer and God's promises to provide for our every need.

Instead, we feel we have to kick and scream and fight and scratch to get what we want. And the bottom line is we don't. The bottom line is God is always in control, He is always looking out for our interests. The bottom line is:

**But seek his kingdom, and these things
will be given to you as well.**
Luke 12:31

The next time you find yourself in an argument, try to take time out to ask yourself whose rights are you really defending. If the answer comes back "mine," then back off, relax, and let it slide.

But I know it's God's will that I have it.

Fine. Then pray and let God do it. There's no need to haggle or fight. If it's for the best and God wants you to have it, somehow you'll wind up having it. (God is used to getting His way.)

And if you don't get it, then you can rest assured that it wasn't for the best and, in the long run, you'll be happier without it.

It's all very simple. It's not always easy, but it is simple.

PONDERING POINTS

☞ What's your last fight been about?

☞ What would have happened if you hadn't fought for your rights?

☞ What would have happened if God had fought for them instead?

But I Prayed...

When you ask, you do not receive, because you ask with wrong motives, that you may spend what you get on your pleasures.
JAMES 4:3

Have you ever heard this line...

You know, I was a Christian once. Yeah, I used to believe all that stuff. Then one time I prayed that God would do this thing for me—you know, something I really needed and wanted more than anything in the whole world. Anyway, I kept praying and praying, and believing, that's important too. But you know, it never happened. So I figured, forget this. I mean, who needs all the disappointment, right?

Not an unusual argument for someone who thought he'd give Christianity a fling.

But looking at it from God's perspective, it's pretty absurd.

**It's like someone chosen to play pro football
who gets all upset and quits because the coach
won't let him make up the plays.**

We are on God's team. He loves us, protects us, and gives us whatever we need or want—if it's what's best for us. But if it will hurt us or our fellow players, there's no way He's going to give it to us. He loves us too much.

And, despite the rumors, we should keep reminding ourselves that God is not an errand boy. He doesn't owe us a thing. We are the ones who owe Him. We are on His team. We are to play for Him.

Yet so many of our prayers go like this: "Dear Lord… Gimme, gimme, gimme, gimme, gimme, gimme." Then we slap an "in Jesus' name we pray" on it as if it were some sort of postage stamp to ensure delivery, and sit back expecting an answer. I mean if I snap my fingers, the least God can do is jump, right?

What about checking on what *He* would have us pray for?

Don't get me wrong. God loves giving to His kids—just as a good, earthly father loves delighting his children with special gifts. But if our prayers are only full of selfish desires, or if they're for things that would hurt our growth or prevent us from winning the game, rest assured His love for us is too great to let us have our way.

If we pray and believe for chocolate fudge sundaes three meals a day, seven days a week, chances are we may wind up a little disappointed.

PONDERING POINTS

☞ What percentage of your prayers are for what you want?

☞ What percentage of your prayers are for what God wants?

World Friendship = God Hatred

*You adulteresses, do you not know that friendship with the world is hostility toward God? Therefore whoever wishes to be a friend of the world makes himself an enemy of God. Or do you think that the Scripture speaks to no purpose: "He jealously desires the Spirit which He has made to dwell in us"? But He gives a greater grace. Therefore it says, "G*OD IS OPPOSED TO THE PROUD, BUT GIVES GRACE TO THE HUMBLE."
JAMES 4:4-6 NASB

James is still pretty bummed over Christians who think they can use God to get whatever they want, that Christianity is just another way to *get* instead of to *give*. It's as though they've completely forgotten what Jesus said: "If anyone would come after me, he must *deny* himself and take up his cross and follow me" (Matthew 16:24).

**Denying self—that's part of what
being a Christian is all about.**

It's not about praying so you can have what Satan is dangling in front of everybody else. And it's not about compromising with the world so you can remain its best buddy or lover.

You cannot have a foot in both kingdoms. It's either one or the other.

We have one Husband, one Lover. He is Jesus Christ. To still be chasing after the world or rolling around in its bed of pleasures is equivalent to committing adultery.

God paid a great price for us—His life. And we are so precious, so dear to Him, that He "jealously" desires us. It's interesting, God is never afraid to use the word "jealous" when referring to His feelings about us. In fact, He uses it again and again in the Old Testament to demonstrate how deep His love is. That's how intense it is, how demanding.

It is NOT God *and* the world.
It is God *or* the world.

But if His love is that intense and that demanding, how can you possibly meet its demands?

A good question, and one that James immediately goes on to answer: "He gives a greater grace" (verse 6). God will never make a demand of you without giving greater grace to accomplish it. He will never ask you to do anything until He gives you the power to do it.

If there is something in this world that you just can't seem to let go of, something that rivals your love for God (or at least your willingness to obey Him), then go to Him.

Humbly ask for help.

If you're sincere, that help will always come.

Always.

PONDERING POINTS

☞ What are God's rivals in your life?

☞ What are you going to do about them?

Breaking the World's Grip

Submit yourselves, then, to God. Resist the devil, and he will flee from you. Come near to God and he will come near to you. Wash your hands, you sinners, and purify your hearts, you double-minded. Grieve, mourn and wail. Change your laughter to mourning and your joy to gloom. Humble yourselves before the Lord, and he will lift you up.
JAMES 4:7-10

Breaking the world's hold on your life is not an easy thing. It can be painful, frustrating, and exhausting.

But it can be done. Say you have that thing, that habit, that relationship that you just can't seem to let go of. In fact, it may be so strong you're not quite sure you *want* to let go. What do you do?

First, go to God. Admit the situation, admit that it's wrong. (Sometimes admitting you're wrong and humbling yourself can be the toughest part of the whole process.)

Second, ask for forgiveness. Remember, God paid an incredible price to forgive you. He killed His one and only Son. That's a lot. And that price covers everything. Everything.

Third, ask for the help to let go. If it's something you know you should drop but you really don't want to, then ask that He help you to *want* to let go. This third step is turning your free will over to Him (submitting) so He has permission to get started. And rest assured, the moment that prayer comes out of your mouth, He'll begin His work.

The final step is putting your faith into action. Remember, godly faith is a two-part process—believing and doing. Well, now comes the doing. You've asked God to give you the strength and/or desire to let go. And now, by faith, believe that you have received it. When temptation arises, believe you've been given the power to resist it. And resist it. "Submit yourselves, then, to God. Resist the devil, and he will flee from you" (James 4:7).

It may turn into a pretty fierce struggle, but if you hang on—if, by faith, you keep claiming you have been given the strength to overcome—the devil will eventually flee.

And you will have won!

But if you want to give in, if you want to fail, you will. And if your heart is right with the Lord, you'll feel terrible—absolutely rotten about it. In fact, you may find yourself crying and weeping before Him. And that's good!

Say what?

THAT'S GOOD! Giving in to sin is not something to take lightly or joke around about. It is something that should break your heart—it should cause you to come humbly to God, devastated.

It doesn't mean you're any less loved or any less saved. What it does mean is that you're starting to see how putrid and deadly your sin really is in the Lord's eyes.

And once that is accomplished, once you start seeing things as they really are, you can again ask for forgiveness and for strength. And once again He'll be faithful in answering your prayers.

This may also be the time to "confess your sins to each other" (James 5:16) by asking your pastor, youth director, or trusted, mature Christian friend to pray for you. It's true, this might seem embarrassing, but there's tremendous power when more than one believer prays. It will also encourage you to know you're not in it alone. There's tremendous freedom when you expose that deep, dark secret to the light, only to discover that somebody you really respect has had or is having a similar sort of struggle.

Then it's time for the battle again—to "resist the devil." Once again, the decision is all yours—whether you want to give in to defeat or hang on to victory. As always, that final decision is yours.

And if you fail? Then you again go to the Lord with tears and weeping. And again He'll forgive you. And again He'll give you the strength to do battle. And so it goes until finally, eventually, you emerge the victor, the winner.

That doesn't mean temptation won't attack again (and there may even be times you decide to give in). But you have now tasted victory and know it can be yours. You know that the stranglehold has been broken. It's true, the devil will keep returning. But as you keep resisting and winning, he'll come at you less and less until he figures, "What's the use?" and goes someplace else.

There are times this sin-breaking process seems to take forever. But don't grow discouraged. Victory will be yours. He paid too much for you to let you fail. *Together*, the two of you will win.

If you're serious, you will win…always. If you come to the Lord humbly broken, humbly seeking His help, you'll always receive it. Always.

And the time will come when He will be able to raise you up before His angels and all of creation, saying: "Behold...My beloved child...My spotless bride...My victorious warrior!"

PONDERING POINTS

☞ What area or person in your life do you feel enslaved to?

☞ Do you want to be free?

☞ Using the above steps, how will you get freedom?

10
PUT A LID ON IT

Don't Gossip

Do not speak against one another, brethren. He who speaks against a brother, or judges his brother, speaks against the law, and judges the law; but if you judge the law, you are not a doer of the law, but a judge of it. There is only one Lawgiver and Judge, the One who is able to save and to destroy; but who are you who judge your neighbor?
JAMES 4:11,12 NASB

I don't know what it is, but we love talking about other people—especially if it means listening to or "sharing" how they've messed up and aren't meeting our standards. It's like we're so insecure about ourselves that we have to dwell on other people's mistakes.

And unfortunately, some of the worst gossips are…you guessed it, Christians!

But what if it's all true? What if what we're saying about the person is 100 percent fact?

**It makes no difference whether you're telling
the truth or telling lies. If it's speaking negatively
about someone behind their back, it's still gossip.**

*Well, all right, I may gossip a little bit, but, I mean,
it's no big sin—everybody does it, at least a little.*

That's what a lot of people think. And a lot of people
will be in for a real shock when they discover that the sins
they are talking about may be less serious than the one
they're committing by gossiping about them.

It's true. God has a pretty low opinion of people who
slander and gossip. In fact, look at the company He puts
them with:

**Do not be deceived: Neither the sexually immoral
nor idolaters nor adulterers nor male prostitutes
nor homosexual offenders nor thieves nor the greedy
nor drunkards nor *slanderers* nor swindlers
will inherit the kingdom of God.**
1 Corinthians 6:9,10

Those are pretty tough words, and ones we should try
our best to remember. But why is God so down on gossip?

James says it's because gossip goes against the law.
The BIG LAW. The law of love. And when you're passing
along or even listening to juicy tidbits about somebody,
chances are you're not really acting in that person's best
interest.

Now that doesn't mean if you're a Christian that you
just go ahead and ignore it with the attitude of, "Oh, well,
who am I to judge?" On the contrary. Scripture makes it

very plain that if you know a brother is sinning, you are to go to that brother and correct him.

But it must always be done face-to-face and never, *never* behind his back.

The next time you feel the urge to slam someone, use your imagination and pretend his dad is standing right beside you, listening to your every word. Because you know what?

He is.

PONDERING POINTS

☞ Have you seen gossip hurt another?

☞ Next time, what can you personally do to stop such hurt?

Remember the Boss

Come now, you who say, "Today or tomorrow, we shall go to such and such a city, and spend a year there and engage in business and make a profit." Yet you do not know what your life will be like tomorrow. You are just a vapor that appears for a little while and then vanishes away. Instead, you ought to say, "If the Lord wills, we shall live and also do this or that." But as it is, you boast in your arrogance; all such boasting is evil.
JAMES 4:13-16 NASB

James is still on Christians who think their lives are to be lived strictly for themselves. They make all these plans about how they're going to rake in the bucks but don't give a second thought as to whether it's something God wants them to do.

The truth is, they don't know what tomorrow will bring. They can brag and boast about their great plans and how successful they're going to be. But without God, their lives are nothing more than "vapor."

The same is true with us. We plan on this college or that marriage or such and such a career. And that's all well and good. It doesn't hurt to plan for the future, to give a little thought as to what would make us happy or how we can best put our talents to use.

**But as we make those plans,
let's remember who we're really living for.**

Our lives are no longer ours, but His. Chances are He just might want a say in what we do.

Someone once said life is what happens when we're busy pursuing other plans.

That can be very true, especially for Christians. Yes, make your plans, do what you think God would have you do, but always keep your ear tilted toward heaven to see if He would have you make any midcourse corrections.

Because, when you do, you'll always be in the center of God's will. Even when you don't feel like it, you'll be there. Remember, God is used to having His way.

PONDERING POINTS

☞ When is planning ahead good?

☞ When is it bad?

Live or Die

Anyone, then, who knows the good he ought to do and doesn't do it, sins.
JAMES 4:17

James has just spent a long time laying it all out for us—telling us what to do, what not to do, explaining how God expects us to behave. Basically the book of James is about how Jesus expects us to live our lives.

Now he gets to the nitty-gritty:

If you don't do it, you sin.

Hard? Inflexible? Unyielding?

Yes.

But let's put the shoe on the other foot. Say you had a child, a child that meant more to you than your very life. You created a wonderful environment for that child to grow and mature, hoping that someday she would help you rule it. But there is one problem. Somebody out there wants to destroy your child. In fact, he has buried land mines everywhere he can think of in an effort to blow up your loved one.

As a parent, wouldn't you do everything in your power to protect your baby? You might even give her a detailed map of the area, showing exactly where she could walk and where she couldn't—a map that showed precisely where those land mines were hidden so she wouldn't accidentally step on one and blow herself up. That's exactly what this letter from James is.

It's a map from God our Father to keep His kids from stepping onto Satan's land mines.

If we follow it, we're safe. If we choose to go our own ways, to sin, we're eventually going to be dead. It's as simple as that.

The map is for us. God gets nothing out of the deal except the joy of seeing us safe and happy. We're the ones it is designed for. And we're the ones who make the ultimate decision as to whether we want to follow it and live—or go our own way, and die.

PONDERING POINTS

☞ What land mines has God warned you about recently?

11
MONEY, PATIENCE, AND TRUTH

More on the Rich

Now listen, you rich people, weep and wail because of the misery that is coming upon you. Your wealth has rotted, and moths have eaten your clothes. Your gold and silver are corroded. Their corrosion will testify against you and eat your flesh like fire. You have hoarded wealth in the last days. Look! The wages you failed to pay the workmen who mowed your fields are crying out against you. The cries of the harvesters have reached the ears of the Lord Almighty. You have lived on earth in luxury and self-indulgence. You have fattened yourselves in the day of slaughter. You have condemned and murdered innocent men, who were not opposing you.
JAMES 5:1-6

Wow! Talk about harsh words.

The rich are told to "weep and wail" because of the judgment that will be coming down on them. He's not talking a little tear here or there—he's talking screams of agony.

Why?

Because instead of using their wealth to help others, instead of resolving in their hearts to let God do with it as He pleases, they just keep storing it up and hoarding it. In fact, their gold and silver corrode from lack of use. And that corrosion will be a testimony against them, eating their flesh like fire.

And if that's not bad enough, some of the rich are actually ripping off the poor. As if they didn't have enough wealth, they actually cheat or refuse to pay their workers what is due. These are the actions that cry out against them.

They live lives of "luxury and self-indulgence," completely unaware that they are just fattening themselves up for the "day of slaughter."

Finally, James says, they have actually "condemned and murdered innocent men." A pretty tough accusation—until you stop to consider that a third of our world is starving to death while many of the rich just sit back and hang on to their money. It's sad that in a very real way they *have* condemned and murdered the innocent.

> **When our Lord blesses with wealth,**
> **He expects that wealth to be used.**
> **He does not expect it to be hoarded.**
> **It serves no one that way.**

It's as if He looks on the needy as parched, desert ground in desperate need of water and upon our wealth as the water that can save them.

Now don't panic. That doesn't mean you have to suffer or do without. All it means is that you should become a type of irrigation pipe, a pipe that enjoys God's wealth as you allow Him to flow His wealth through you to bless others.

A pretty ingenious plan when you stop to think about it. Even though you're passing the water on, you'll be able to drink from it because it will be flowing through you. Yet at the same time, others will also be able to use it.

You are the pipe. All you have to do is take what you need and allow the rest to pass through.

And since God promises to supply "abundantly," you should have no worries. That water will always be there. In fact, we read in Luke 6:38 that Jesus said the more you give, the more you'll receive (that is, the more you allow to flow through you, the greater and faster will be the flow).

The trouble comes when the self-centered rich decide they want to dam up the flow so they can make a lake for their yachts. Or, it's sadder still when the Christian starts to distrust God. He starts fearing that the Lord will shut off the supply, so he'd better clog up the pipe and hoard the water for himself—just in case the Supplier messed up, just in case He can't really be trusted.

And the final result? Water that nobody can use. Water that keeps backing up and stagnating until it becomes so foul that no one can drink it.

While at the same time, the people at the other end of the pipe are dying of thirst.

While at the same time those innocent ones are being "condemned and murdered."

PONDERING POINTS

☞ What percentage of your money do you spend on yourself?

☞ What percentage of your money do you spend on God?

Hang On

Be patient, therefore, brethren, until the coming of the Lord. Behold, the farmer waits for the precious produce of the soil, being patient about it, until it gets the early and late rains. You too be patient; strengthen your hearts, for the coming of the Lord is at hand. Do not complain, brethren, against one another, that you yourselves may not be judged; behold, the Judge is standing right at the door.
JAMES 5:7-9 NASB

There was a certain city slicker who thought he'd try his hand at raising corn. It couldn't be too tough. I mean, if farmers could do it, anybody could, right?

So he bought 40 acres, plowed it, and planted the seeds. It was hard work—a lot harder than he had seen in the movies—but he loved corn on the cob and figured it was worth it.

But to his great dismay, when he woke up the following morning, he saw nothing. The ground looked exactly as it had the day before. Here he had gone to all that work, waited a whole 24 hours, and for what? Nothing. There was no corn to be found.

Local folks tried to explain that he'd have to wait through the entire summer. But he knew better.

After all, back home behind those sparkling tile counters it only took 45 seconds for someone to produce a Big Mac, and that had meat, lettuce, tomatoes, and everything.

But he was a patient man and gave it another day. Then another. Finally, by the end of the week, he was so frustrated that he sold the land and moved back to the city where they didn't take all day to get something done.

The same is true with us and good works. If corn, which can be eaten in a matter of minutes and then is gone, takes an entire summer to raise, how much longer will our good works, which last an eternity, take before they mature and provide us with a harvest?

But we live in an age of instant everything. If we don't see the rewards within a few days or even weeks, we grow discouraged.

That's why James is rooting us on.

Hang in there. Strengthen your heart. Don't give up. The Great Rewarder is coming—He's just around the corner. Every good deed and every selfless act is being recorded.

Not one deed, not a single one, will be forgotten. Each will be rewarded.

In the meantime, don't grow discouraged—especially with one another. If you do a good deed for a brother and he takes it for granted or even winds up hurting you, don't grumble or be resentful. Just figure he's growing and maturing in Christ, and maybe the next time he'll treat you like a human being. Maybe...

Yeah, but he's a Christian, so he's supposed to know better.

That's right. But when was the last time you knew what you should do and didn't do it?

We're all human, and we're all under construction. Let's give each other a break, especially with the Boss standing just outside getting ready to enter.

All this to say: Don't give up on doing good and reaching out to others, even if it means getting nothing at first. It may take days, weeks, even years before you see any harvest from the love. But it will always come.

Keep investing in that heavenly bank account. Hang on and wait. It may seem to take forever before your investment reaches full maturity. But, believe me, the dividends will be astronomical. In fact, you could say the interest rates will be out of this world.

PONDERING POINTS

☞ What deeds have you done that weren't rewarded until later?

☞ What deeds feel like they'll never be rewarded?

☞ What does God say about them?

Persevere

Brothers, as an example of patience in the face of suffering, take the prophets who spoke in the name of the Lord. As you know, we consider blessed those who have persevered. You have heard of Job's perseverance and have seen what the Lord finally brought about. The Lord is full of compassion and mercy.
JAMES 5:10,11

In the old days, prophets were often ridiculed, beaten, tortured, imprisoned, and killed. Once they decided to follow the Lord they would hang on and nothing, absolutely *nothing* would make them let go.

According to the book of Revelation, that time will again return, a time when the beast will be "given power to make war against the saints and to conquer them" (Revelation 13:7).

There will be pain, suffering, and death for those who have made up their minds to follow the Lord.

In some countries a time of suffering is already happening. Because they dare to obey Christ, men and women in China and in some Muslim countries are harassed, some are imprisoned, and some even have their children torn away from them. In other countries with civil unrest, pastors have been gunned down in front of their own churches.

And Jesus says that someday such persecution will be worldwide.

But once again, God will never ask us to do something unless He gives us the power to do it. The faith of those people being persecuted today is awesome. Some are like spiritual giants. And if we're around when that time of persecution comes, rest assured He'll also give us the faith to endure it.

In fact, some believe that we're being trained for those times right now. That may be why He's taking us through a faith workout program—to build our faith muscles, to make us stronger, to prepare us. So when the time comes, we'll be able to endure and survive.

And the rewards are great:

> **To him who overcomes, I will give the right to sit with me on my throne, just as I overcame and sat down with my Father on his throne.**
> Revelation 3:21

No matter what pain or wounds we receive in the overcoming, no matter what our losses are in the battle (either now or in the future), if we hang on and endure, we'll receive several times the blessings when it's all over. Job is probably the best example. Satan threw everything he had at him. He wiped out all of his possessions, killed all of his children, and covered him with boils from head to foot. But Job hung on.

And when it was all over, Job not only emerged with a closer, more intimate relationship with God, but he was actually given *double* of everything he had in the first place. How much more should we persevere and hang on, we who have been promised rulership with the Creator of the universe.

Because God always prevails. *Always.*

We may get stomped on from time to time. We may lose a battle now and then. But if we persevere, we'll eventually wind up the victors, sitting with our King on His throne.

**And who is the one who overcomes the world,
but he who believes that Jesus is the Son of God?**
1 John 5:5 NASB

PONDERING POINTS

☞ What type of persecution have you faced for your faith?

☞ What type of persecution could you expect in the future?

Living Integrity

But above all, my brethren, do not swear, either by heaven or by earth or with any other oath; but let your yes be yes, and your no, no; so that you may not fall under judgment.
JAMES 5:12 NASB

Back in James' day there was so much dishonesty that in order to convince someone you were telling the truth you had to swear it was true before God or heaven or whatever. In fact, it got to be so bad that Jesus said:

**Do not swear at all: either by heaven,
for it is God's throne; or by the earth,
for it is his footstool; or by Jerusalem, for it is
the city of the Great King. And do not swear by your
head, for you cannot make even one hair white or black.
Simply let your "Yes" be "Yes," and your "No," "No";
anything beyond this comes from the evil one.**
Matthew 5:34-37

But how does this apply to today? A good question.

Some devout Christians believe that it applies literally—that they are never to take any oath, whether in court or in joining an organization or whatever. They simply make it clear that they believe taking an oath is against what Jesus teaches; when they say yes, they mean yes, and when they say no, they mean no.

Other dedicated believers feel that Jesus and James were addressing a particular problem of that day and that it no longer applies to our time and culture.

But, regardless of the different convictions on this matter, we can all agree on one thing:

God gives us the ability to lead lives so pure and so honest that we no longer need to go through verbal gymnastics to convince people we are telling the truth.

We should practice such honesty and integrity throughout our day-to-day existence that our reputations, our very lives, should be enough to convince others we are of the truth and that what comes out of our mouths will only be the truth.

PONDERING POINTS

☞ How do you stack up in the honesty department?

☞ What's the last lie you've told?

☞ As far as God is concerned, is there ever a good reason to lie?

12
TEAM WORKOUT

Prayer Power

*Is any one of you in trouble? He should pray. Is anyone happy?
Let him sing songs of praise. Is any one of you sick? He should
call the elders of the church to pray over him and anoint him
with oil in the name of the Lord. And the prayer offered in faith
will make the sick person well; the Lord will raise him up. If he
has sinned, he will be forgiven. Therefore confess your sins to
each other and pray for each other so that you may be healed.
The prayer of a righteous man is powerful and effective.*
JAMES 5:13-16

There's lots here. But everything James said can be
boiled down to one word:

FAITH.

It is FAITH in Jesus Christ that gives us eternal life.
Jesus said, "I am the resurrection and the life. He who

believes in me will live, even though he dies; and whoever lives and believes in me will never die" (John 11:25,26).

It is FAITH that acts as a shield, protecting us from whatever the enemy may try to throw our way. "In addition to all this, take up the shield of faith, with which you can extinguish all the flaming arrows of the evil one" (Ephesians 6:16).

It is FAITH that enables us to push aside whatever mountain stands before us. Jesus said, "I tell you the truth, if you have faith as small as a mustard seed, you can say to this mountain, 'Move from here to there' and it will move. Nothing will be impossible for you" (Matthew 17:20).

In fact:

Without faith it is impossible to please God.
Hebrews 11:6

Is it any wonder that James adds, "The prayer offered in faith will make the sick person well"?

It's funny...with so much scientific and medical technology, we've almost forgotten that God is still in the healing business. He hasn't gone anywhere. He's never resigned. He's not on vacation. He's right here. And James is quite serious when he challenges us to call on God for help. If you're sick, contact the elders of your church and have them pray for you in faith. And if you can't get any elders, then at least find some other mature believers who can pray...*in faith*.

For "the prayer of a righteous man is powerful and effective" (James 5:16).

In the same verse he says, "Confess your sins to each other and pray for each other so that you may be healed."

The healing here may be physical (some sins do bring physical sickness). But it may also refer to "spiritual sickness."

If there is a sin that keeps haunting you, that keeps hanging on, one way you might get rid of it is to confess it to someone else. We've mentioned this before, but the point cannot be overemphasized.

**Satan loves to work in the dark.
He loves for you to keep your sins secret.**

He rejoices in the hopelessness and despair that come over you when you think you're the only one caught in a particular sin—when you think you're some sort of spiritual reject and that no one could possibly love you if you were found out.

And he's thrilled when you try to fight the battle all by yourself. Because then he usually wins.

But when you're joined together with other mature believers whom you trust, when the power of their prayers is united with yours, then the darkness doesn't have a chance. When you open the door to your deepest, darkest secrets and let the light flood in, then darkness has no place to hide. It can do nothing but disappear.

Whether the battle is physical or spiritual, go to one another. Trust one another. Pray with one another. Because when you do, all hell shudders. Because when you do, the enemy has to step aside and let you claim the land.

PONDERING POINTS

☞ What are some of your "secret battles"?

☞ Can you think of a *mature* Christian you can pray with about them?

More on Faith

Elijah was a man just like us. He prayed earnestly that it would not rain, and it did not rain on the land for three and a half years. Again he prayed, and the heavens gave rain, and the earth produced its crops.
JAMES 5:17,18

Lots of people look at Jesus' promise, "You may ask me for anything in my name, and I will do it" (John 14:14), as a blank check. "Great," they say. "That means I can have anything I want—unlimited wealth, fame, popularity, a couple dozen mansions, and let's not forget those 15 BMW convertibles. All I have to do is believe hard enough."

Not quite.

"Ask me for anything *in my name.*" That doesn't mean just ending a prayer with a quick "in Jesus' name, amen." Again, that phrase is not some postage stamp that we slap onto our prayers to make sure they get delivered.

It means praying about a situation as Jesus would pray, as if we were representing Him here on earth.

An ambassador to a foreign country doesn't speak on his own behalf, but he speaks *in the name* of the country he represents. He finds out what his country wants and then proclaims it.

The same is true with us. We pray and wait on the Lord until we think we know what is best. Then in faith, without doubting, we begin to pray it into existence.

But the answer doesn't always come overnight.

Elijah was a good example. He didn't have too much trouble stopping the rain. But when he prayed for it to start again, three and a half years later, he got zip. Nothing. In fact, there wasn't a cloud to be seen. He could have given up, thrown up his hands, and walked away. But instead, he kept on praying…and praying…and praying… until finally, a little cloud began to form. And he kept at it, praying his heart out, until, at last there was a tremendous downpour.

Like Elijah, we're to pray, believing—no matter how impossible it looks, no matter how long it may take.

Sometimes those waiting periods are for God to make it more clear to us what He really wants. Sometimes they're out-and-out warfare against the devil. And sometimes they're just tests. But once we know His will and begin to pray, we should never give up—*never.*

Even though there isn't a cloud in the sky, keep on praying.

There's a true story of a man who dreamed he had died and gone to heaven. He and Jesus were walking down the long hallway of his life, looking at the dozens of doors he had opened through his persistent prayers.

"But what about all those?" the man asked, pointing down the hallway to hundreds of other doors, tightly sealed.

"Those," Jesus sadly replied, "are the prayers you wouldn't let Me answer."

PONDERING POINTS

☞ What areas are difficult for you to trust God in?

☞ If you were God, what would you do to help you grow in those areas?

We're All in This Together

My brethren, if any among you strays from the truth, and one turns him back, let him know that he who turns a sinner from the error of his way will save his soul from death, and will cover a multitude of sins.
JAMES 5:19,20 NASB

James ends the book with another reminder that we're not in this life alone.

Through James, God lays down a lot of clear-cut rights and wrongs—crystal-clear guidelines on how to become "mature and complete, not lacking anything."

The workout may be tough, the battle against the enemy fierce. But the important thing to keep in mind is:

We are not in this alone.

First, we have the Coach, who's right there on the field with us, rooting us on, encouraging us, running along beside us. In fact, He's actually living *inside* us—giving us the power and ability to run that extra lap, to break that particular sin, to reach out and love that unlovable one.

Second, we've got each other. As believers we're all on the same team, working toward the same goal. If one suffers, we all suffer; if one wins, we all win.

In fact, in Ephesians 6, where Paul wrote about the shield of faith, there's a good chance he was thinking of the Roman shield. It was rectangular and designed to lock in with all the other shields to form a vast, impregnable wall. It worked best only when used with the others.

Unfortunately, many of us think Christianity is a Lone Ranger type of thing—as if we can go out there and overcome the enemy all by ourselves. Nothing can be further from the truth. We need each other. Christ has *one* body and *one* bride.

Not me…

Not you…

…us.

There are plenty of times when we get hurt, when we want to walk away from it all, when we're sure there's no way God can work with a bunch of bozos who claim they're Christians. But hang in there.

Those times of hurt and rejection are just the enemy's way of trying to single you out from the herd so he can go in for the kill.

Don't fall for it.

We are responsible for each other. And when we stand *together* in faith, nothing can get in our way. When we stand together, whole and complete, not even the gates of hell can remain before us.

Wholeness and maturity are what Jesus Christ desires for our lives. His goal for us is:

**That we may become victors, winners, overcomers.
That you and I may lack absolutely nothing.**

Hang in there. Let Him have His way. It will happen. In fact, whether you feel it or not…

… it's happening even now.

PONDERING POINTS

☞ What areas do you think God wants to work on in your character?

☞ Will you let Him?

Other Good
Harvest House Reading

The Power of a Praying® Teen
Stormie Omartian

Along with Scripture verses and true stories of teens in action, *The Power of a Praying® Teen* addresses key issues you face, including purity, peer pressure, insecurity, body and self-image, and friendships.

A Young Man After God's Own Heart
Jim George

On this radical journey of faith, you'll explore God's wisdom, biblical principles, and powerful insights from the life of King David. You'll discover God's amazing will, gear up for serving God, and build meaningful friendships.

A Young Woman After God's Own Heart
Elizabeth George

This teen version of *A Woman After God's Own Heart®* shares the intentions and blessings of God's heart with you. You'll discover His priorities for your life, including prayer, submission, faithfulness, and joy.

The Bondage Breaker® Youth Edition
Neil Anderson and Dave Park

Helping you strip away superficiality and live a Christ-centered life, Neil and Dave offer steps for breaking sinful habits; increasing confidence that through Christ sin wields no power; and relying on the Holy Spirit for guidance.

Purity Under Pressure
Neil Anderson and Dave Park

Few things cause as much confusion and conflict as the issue of sexual purity. In a reassuring style, Neil and Dave present spiritual truths behind sexual temptations and provide simple ways to develop godly relationships.